AUTHOR-ITY
Fiona Jones

PUBLISH YOUR BOOK
INCREASE YOUR CREDIBILITY
EXPAND YOUR BUSINESS

Disclaimer

All the information, techniques, skills and concepts contained within this publication are of the nature of general comment only and are not in any way recommended as individual advice. The intent is to offer a variety of information to provide a wider range of choices now and in the future, recognising that we all have widely diverse circumstances and viewpoints.

Should any reader choose to make use of the information contained herein, this is their decision and the author and publishers do not assume any responsibilities whatsoever under any condition or circumstances. It is recommended that the reader obtain their own independent advice.

First Edition 2017

Copyright © 2017 by Fiona Jones

National Library of Australia

Cataloguing-in-Publication entry:
Creator: Jones, Fiona, author.
Title: Author-ity : Publish Your Book | Increase Your Credibility | Expand Your Business / Fiona Jones.

ISBN: 9781925471144 (paperback)
ISBN: 9781925471151 (e-book)

Subjects: Authorship.
Authorship--Marketing.
Publishers and publishing.
Success in business.

Dewey Number: 808.02

Published by Author Express
www.authorexpress.com
publish@authorexpress.com

|Author|

...A person who creates or publishes a plan, idea or a book.

| Author-ity|

...A person with influence and credibility, who is known in their niche and trusted by their clients, customers and industry experts.

Want to be a Published Author?

Writing and publishing your very own book doesn't have to be difficult. You just need to have a message to share.

At Author Express, we love turning your publishing dreams into a reality. We're here to help you if you're:

- ▸ *A Difference Maker*: You have a message to share that will make a difference in the world
- ▸ *A Business Owner:* The best business card on the planet is a book
- ▸ *A Writer*: You've written a book and just want to know the most effective way to publish it

We would love to help!

In addition to this book grab some author kickstarter bonuses now at: www.authorexpress.com/start

Author Express
From Inspiration To Publication In 5 Simple Steps

Contents

FOREWORD

I first met Fiona when she interviewed me for her book, *Millionaire Motivators*, in 2011. I loved her work and was impressed with her as an authority in the industry, after learning how she'd helped so many people become published authors.I was further impressed when she also helped me become a best-selling author.

Within the pages of this book, Fiona reveals the process of to how to go about starting a business with a book and growing it into digital online products and high-ticket items. I've personally witnessed her do this and can say with complete certainty that she walks her talk. It's why several years ago I flew to meet with Fiona about launching a product to help our community publish their books and become authors.

The end result is that we became business partners and founded Author Express.

The education Fiona provides is way more than how to write a book. She likes to think big and have her authors gain clarity and a greater vision for what's possible, way beyond the book itself.I remember reading once that when you buy a book, you're paying for the ink and the paper, but the ideas that are priceless are usually free.

Getting your message to millions of people, and delivering it in an effective way without having to be present, is one of the delivery methods we teach at Authentic Education. There are two highly effective ways to do that:

1. Become an author.
2. Create a digital product people can download on the internet and transmit digitally.

The advice in this book is priceless, and Fiona has spilled the beans on how she, and many of her clients, have gone on to build a business and become an author-ity in their niche, while doing what they love.

There has never been an easier time in history to make this happen. All you need to do is connect what you love to do with your inner vision of who you imagine your future self to be, and everything will accelerate dramatically.

Benjamin J Harvey
Co-Founder of Authentic Education
www.authenticeducation.com.au

INTRODUCTION

Everyday people, speakers, trainers, consultants, healers and coaches are positioning themselves and becoming highly paid experts by sharing their story, message and expertise in a published book to a public thirsty for their knowledge.

Some names that may be instantly recognisable to you are Anthony Robbins, Brian Tracy, Steven Covey, Dr John Demartini, Deepak Chopra and Dr Wayne Dyer. These people have been mentors to millions, because they came to be known as authorities in their industry, all due to publishing a book. And once they realised the power of publishing, they wrote multiple books to fast track their success.

I'm sure you've had unique experiences you'd love to share with others and make a difference in their lives, while also amassing a fortune doing it. You're reading this book right now, because you want to know how to become known in your niche by publishing a book. In other words, you want to be an *authority*. Imagine someone Googling your name and seeing you're a published author. I intend to help you peel back the curtain on a bigger vision for your book.

After years of trying to get noticed, many of my clients have been featured on radio, national television, newspapers and magazines and been invited speakers. Their manuscript is on shelves in bookstores, achieving number one best-seller status. They're even able to raise their fees and no longer need to compete within their industry. Their book has become their pedestal.

My authors have attracted high-paying clients and joint-venture partnerships. By becoming a published author, they're leaving a legacy. You can't put a price on that experience.

This is the power of being a published author.

Clarity and Author-ity

At one time, trying to promote yourself and your business by writing a book was a bit of a novelty. Now, it's a must-have. If a potential client is choosing between your services and those of someone who's written a book on the subject, I think you can guess who they'd choose. People want to work with the person who wrote the book. It gives you the instant *author-ity* and credibility factor and sets you up as an expert. Then you can go about building a brand or business around it. These days, a book is almost as expected as a website.

Are you struggling to attract clients? You can fast track the path to success and attract quality clients and customers to your business just by publishing. A book can be your brand accelerator.

I've become an *author-ity* in my niche of publishing. Clients and business opportunities come to me. People read a book series I've published and want to do the same with their own series on their area of expertise. Or they just want to add the title of author to their resume, and they know I can help by getting them published. I've been privileged to have joint-venture partnerships with likeminded people who have the ideal client base for my services. Almost everyone interviewed on a podcast is an author. It's because their book opens them up to a broad audience and is easy to build a discussion around.

The New Rules of Publishing

The rules of publishing have changed. Technology has completely disrupted the industry. In fact, there's never been a better time to publish. It no longer takes years for the process to occur. You can even be in control of every aspect of your book and have complete ownership of it.

Gone are the days of sending off your manuscript to multiple publishers, only to have it rejected. Now you can publish like the pros, using the exact platforms the big publishers do. With the introduction of the internet and technology, anyone can now publish a book from their kitchen table. In a matter of months you can go from an idea to published author. One click of a button, and someone on the other side of the world can order your book in multiple formats from Amazon, Booktopia, Book Depository and numerous other online retailers. Transactions like these are happening millions of times a day. In fact, I run my entire publishing company with a laptop computer and an internet connection from wherever I am in the world.

Traditionally, word of mouth has been the best marketing tool for authors, but due to technology, it's been amplified. Social media, blogs, forums, YouTube and online bookstores means everyday people can get exposure and market reach that in the past was only available to those with big budgets who could pay to get the word out on traditional media.

Your Book is Your Business Card

What may not be evident is that most successful manuscripts often have nothing to do how many copies of the book are sold. The success is in the business behind it. Doing it right and producing a professionally published book means you'll be known as the *author-ity* in your laneway. By using your book as your brochure and business card to introduce yourself, your business and the products and services you offer, you create a backend. But that's only if you provide great value to the reader and answer the questions they want answered. Your book must contain quality content all by itself, while at the same time act as an invitation for your reader to further their relationship with you and your business.

This book is not about turning a successful businessperson into a *writer*. To date, only one of my clients has been a professional writer. It's more important to get the knowledge and expertise you already have between your ears, also known as your *intellectual property* (IP), and organising it in a way that people will get to know you. After all, they want to work with those they know, like and trust, and there's no better way of accomplishing this than through a book.

Daniel Priestley, author of the books *Key Person of Influence* and *Oversubscribed*, explains the 10|4|7 concept. Broken down to its essence, for people to build trust and professional rapport, they need ten touchpoints over four different mediums that totals seven hours of time invested with you, before they will purchase your product or service. This doesn't mean a one-time small purchase but investing in a coaching package, retreat, bootcamp, program or hiring you as a consultant. An example of the time someone would need to allot would be reading four of your blogs, watching some YouTube videos of you discussing your topic, reading your Facebook posts or perhaps listening to a podcast.

As I read about the 10|4|7 concept, I had a massive lightbulb moment. I knew without a doubt that anyone who wanted to have more clients, customers, cashflow and credibility, had to become an author. A key part of the KPI program is that you *must* publish. Why? Because if a person reads multiple chapters of your book, then *boom*! That's seven hours of their time they've devoted to you. They're reading in their home, on the train or bus, on holidays and in bed. There's no better way to build trust and rapport without being in the same room. This is the ultimate leverage. From your book you can then link them to your podcast, YouTube videos, a free download and your blogs. Again, these are your touchpoints that will make them eager to do business with you.

A book is an asset you create once and leverage thereafter. It's a time saver. Instead of having endless meetings or phone conversations repeating the same information, your potential client can read your book, get all of the preliminary information, and begin their relationship with you as a paying client or customer. In other words, the book has done the qualifying for you.

Most entrepreneurs have read the book *Rich Dad Poor Dad*. by Robert Kiyosaki. I employ this as an example of using a book as a brochure or business card. Kiyosaki is not an author.

He's a businessman who co-authored a book. His twenty-dollar self-published book was written as a brochure for the three-hundred-dollar board game he created. Are you starting to understand this concept now?

The book got him media attention, radio and TV interviews, and eventually on the *New York Times* best-seller list for years. Despite the amount of money he made from book sales, the real money was in his board game, which then led customers to his coaching programs, seminars and events. This business model isn't just reserved for the Robert Kyosakis of the world. You don't even have to sell any books to be successful. Attempting to sell copies of your book is for amateurs. Everyday people become successful by using their book to boost their business and market themselves as the go-to person in their industry.

I'm Not a Writer

So, you say you can't become an author, because you're not a writer. Neither am I! People just presume because you're a published author you're also a writer. Nothing could be further from the truth. The most successful entrepreneurs focus on what they do well and outsource the rest or have experts in their team. They don't even need to know how to put together a grammatically perfect sentence. My young daughter knows more about the structure and grammar of writing than I do.

There's a big difference between being a writer and being an author, and not being one doesn't mean you can't be the other.

Recently, my editor made a notation that something I'd written contained a *dangling participle*.

I admit I had to look it up.

You don't have to know the difference between a noun or verb, or terminology that sounds like you need immediate medical attention. This should be a huge relief to many people who are told to be something or someone they're not. Let me repeat: you don't have to be a writer to become an author.

Paperback or Digital?

Having a physical, professionally published book is important. An electronic book of any kind turned into a print book isn't good enough and in fact can damage your brand by repelling people.

There was a big buzz when digital publishing came into play, because the barrier to entry was minimal. This meant anyone with a computer and access to the internet could publish an e-book. If you want to be taken seriously as a professional in your field, you need a professionally published book that can be sent to current and prospective clients, media and event organisers seeking speakers and potential joint-venture partners. Posting a physical book will make you stand out from the crowd. It might sound easy to send an email with your book attached, but many people won't bother to download a large attachment.

Of course, extending your audience reach means having your book available in other formats. Someone being able to zap your book onto their phone or tablet and read it anywhere, is a great convenience. In fact, I'm a fan of these mediums in conjunction with a professionally published book.

When you're at a networking event, telling someone to go and download your e-book, isn't nearly as impressive as having a professionally published book you *authorgraph* personally, that includes your mobile number.

Maybe you've written a book on relationships, and you want to send it to a journalist in order to gain media attention. How much more impressive would it be to send it in a heart-shaped box, perhaps with some chocolates, rather than an impersonal email instructing them to download a PDF? This is exactly what one of my clients did to great success.

While book lovers will cringe just thinking about it, if you've written a how-to book, your readers will want to make notes in the margins, highlight and even dog-ear the pages. I know I do. I see the book as a learning tool I want to revisit and not a museum piece. I never used to light my candles, but now I let them burn. I want to use everything I own. After all, isn't that the point of life? To enjoy it? Stop locking away your possessions.

While your readers will have a preference as to how they consume your book, you must publish to raise your *author-ity* in your niche. In fact, it's a MUST.

Investing in Your Future

Are you interested in having a quality professionally published book that's an asset you create once and leverage for years to come, just like a website? You should, as it can become an integral part of your personal brand. In creating your book you will gain incredible clarity around your business, whether you're a veteran or just starting out. Aside from perhaps having a child, it can be one of the most fulfilling experiences in your life. The time investment in going through the process of becoming an author is one of the best personal development courses available. You can fully understand this feeling once you hold your book in your hands, hot off the press.

ABOUT THIS BOOK

Most people I meet tell me publishing a book is on their bucket list. Although my subtitle, *Publish Your Book, Increase Your Credibility, Expand your Business* alludes to publishing a book in your area of expertise to position yourself and become an authority, this information can be used for any size or genre of book. In fact, after publishing their "business" book, my clients will often go on and publish what can be termed their *passion project*, which can be a children's book, or even a fiction novel or novella. By following the action steps I've outlined, you can create a blueprint and marketing asset that will elevate you and your business by giving you the *author-ity* factor.

PART ONE
Your Book

"You can't start the next chapter of your life if you keep re-reading the last one. Time to take action and start your book and a new chapter today."

— Author Unknown

WARNING: PROCRASTINATION IS THE SINGLE BIGGEST BOOK KILLER

"Never forget: This very moment, we can change our lives. There never was a moment, and never will be, when we are without the power to alter our destiny. This second, we can turn the tables on resistance. This second, we can sit down and do our work."
— **Steven Pressfield**

You're in danger of never letting your book see the light of day. Procrastination, borne out of fear and perfectionism, stops most people from realising their dream of becoming a published author. The only person stopping you from writing and publishing your book is you.

For every dream you've ever had, you've probably met the dreaded resistance. The voices inside your head that say you aren't up to the task. Well-meaning friends and family who tell you it's a pipe dream and to be more realistic. Resistance can be a powerful force, so you need to recognise it and take action despite its magnetic pull. You might recognise some of these excuses:

- *Who are you to write a book?*
- *You're not an expert.*
- *You don't know enough to write book.*
- *You're not a writer. Who do you think you are?*

This is what the voice of resistance sounds like, and its job is to close you off from inspiration.

In life there are equal and opposite reactions. This means when you take on a new challenge you'll be met with resistance, which is like a force of nature. Knowing and understanding how it pops up in your life will help you put mechanisms in place to push it away and not let it deter you from realising your dream. It's important to remember that the universe conspires to help those who take action, and life rewards action, so don't let resistance prevent you from moving forward. Just start writing, and ignore your old and limiting beliefs that tell you you're not an author.

I experienced this resistance when I set out to write my first book. At first, I didn't want to tell anybody, because years, earlier when I made my first attempt, it wasn't as common an occurrence as it is now. Also, I had a medical background, so everybody saw me in that medical role. For me to say, "I'm writing a book. I'm going to be a published author", I had to push through a lot of barriers I had erected.

What I've learnt is that the only way to overcome resistance is to take action on what will lead you to fulfilling your dream. In this case, go and sit at your keyboard and start typing. There are even programs that allow you to dictate your book.

Just write one word and then another. Before you know it you'll have a sentence, a paragraph, then a page, and by the end of the week, a chapter. Merely taking action will overcome resistance and get you in the flow. Then the thought may come to mind, *Why did I procrastinate for so long?*

The time to write your book is now. All it involves is organising your information, and before you know it, you'll be able to say you're an author. The best part is that you won't only change your life, but the lives of others. Give yourself permission to create your book.

Firsts are always the hardest: first baby, first house, first business and your first book. A lot of the authors I work with go on to create multiple books, because they realise it's much easier once they know how by following the system I'm sharing here.

The best part about becoming an author is the person you become in the process. This is your green light. The time to take action is now.

STEP ONE: PREPARE

"If you fail to plan, you're planning to fail."

Why bother?

I believe everyone has a book inside of them. Most have more than one. Because of your unique experiences, sharing your message could make a difference and help someone who's struggling on their journey. The best way to share your experience and knowledge, and brand your business with you as the *author-ity*, is to write or author a book.

Everyone has a passion story to share with the world. Maybe it's a talent you're proficient at and would love to teach others. You can create a book to build a business or generate more business.

▸ Love cooking? Publish a book and create a cooking school.

▸ Love healing? Publish a book on healing and run a retreat.

▸ Love your profession? Publish a book and become a highly paid speaker and trainer.

▸ Love health and fitness? Publish a book and offer coaching, online programs and licences.

Publishing a book is about getting the information out of your head and onto paper. If it's a legacy and a message you want to leave that will help others long after you're gone, there's a way to get it out of your heart and onto the page. I can help you share your message in a way that's unique, honest and authentic to you.

Start with the End in Mind

The biggest reason most authors don't finish their book and never become published is because they failed to plan or chose a subject they weren't passionate about, so they had no real purpose. Yes, you have a dream of becoming an author, and you want to take action, but the first step is to identify the burning desire inside of you. What story is bursting to get out? Having an understanding that a book is part of building a business begs the question, *What sort of business do you want?*

Along with not having a plan, being unaware of the steps to take or neglecting to have a framework for your book can stop you in your tracks. Every successful person I've interviewed for my *Millionaire* book series has become successful through what I call *FAMMISH*. This is an acronym of the steps you need to take on the path to success. The mere thought of publishing a book can be overwhelming. Having a plan in place, and taking small steps to get there, will make your dream into a reality.

▸ Face the fear

I deal with a lot of people regarding getting their book published, and the common problem I've encountered is a lot of excuses based in fear. Here are a few examples:

What will people say?

This is a common concern, and my answer is always the same: *it's none of your business what other people think of you!* They will have their opinion, and there's absolutely nothing you can do about it.

Savvy authors focus on serving their clients, not wondering what the competition is up to or what others think or say about them. They keep their focus on their mission of helping others.

I don't know anyone

When I first started out, I had nobody to interview. I happened to be at the event where I learnt to write a book only because I was given tickets by my sister who was unable to attend. I had no plans of becoming a published author.

Don't let the small stuff stop you from moving forward. You can no longer use the excuse of not knowing where to start, when you have the entire world at your fingertips. All I did was Google *property experts*, purchase property magazines, and took note of who they featured. Then I contacted them and asked if they'd give me a positive interview that would be featured in my upcoming book.

I don't have any time

Without exception, people have time for what they value. Put the time aside. You can be strategic about the timing.

I have a lot of authors who do a framework and can produce the manuscript in under a week. Others take months and some a year. Work out what you want, but understand your mindset plays a massive role in whatever your endeavour, whether writing a book or starting a business, and nothing beats a tight deadline for motivation.

I chose to write this book when rain was forecast, and my children had exam week. I knew they would be home studying, and I would be indoors due to the rain. This meant the usual craziness wouldn't get in the way. I had a one-week window between major publishing projects, so I had a choice: get it finished or wait six months. I took the opportunity to make it happen instead of hoping for the nebulous "later" that never happens.

What motivated me and kept me on track during the creating and producing of the *Millionaire* book series was having the cover created at the start. Making sure your book cover is on your vision board or computer screen can keep you focussed and on track. You can always make changes later on. That's a minor detail. What's important is getting the words out of your head and onto the page. Everything else can be fine-tuned later.

I don't know where to start

Even the greatest minds who've written classic novels or created an invention, didn't know where to begin. That's normal. When I started in property investing and development, I read books and went to seminars where I found mentors. When I put my first book together, I reverse engineered all of the steps after investing $25,000. Following a proven system and keeping it as simple as possible will move you forward much faster than investing a lot of money and time to figure out someone else's complicated system. This is another way to procrastinate.

When you're embarking on a new venture, and you don't know the next step to take, your primal brain will step in and put up a roadblock. This is the opposite way of making your dream become a reality.

It's too hard and takes too long

This thought pattern is derived from old beliefs. It used to be that a person could take years to write a book, only to have it rejected by a publisher. Those days are over. With new technology it's never been a better time to publish your book without being at the mercy of a big publishing house. Most authors can comfortably go from inspiration to publication in less than a year.

I'm not a writer

I've already told you I'm not a writer, and yet here you are reading my book.

You don't even need to do any writing. I published my first nine books without typing a word. I call this *The book that writes itself* aka *The lazy author method*. My first book paid for itself and made a profit before it was printed. There are a lot of ways to approach publishing your book.

People are writing more than ever before. Though you may not think of it this way, typing out emails, social media posts, blogs and text messages means you're writing more than you think. On a daily basis I see long, interesting Facebook posts and think about how all they have to do is collate them and call it *How I Wrote My Book on Facebook*. Now, there's an idea!

When you set a goal to write a book, the most self-defeating thought to have is, *I have to write an entire book*. It's simply overwhelming. Just write 250 words at a time. You can do that, right?

In fact, you can get a blank Word document right now and prove it to yourself by writing about the first thought that comes to your mind.

There's already a book on my topic

Unless you're an alien beaming down from another planet, it would be impossible to come up with a subject nobody else has written about. Do you think this is the only manuscript in the world on how to publish a book? What do I have that others don't? My expertise and perspective. Nobody else has been in my shoes and had the same experiences I've had.

After working in this industry for over eight years, I wanted to write this book from what I know and share what has worked for me and my clients. When seeking information on a topic, you don't just go to one website or pick up one book, right? That would be short-sighted.

Remember, this isn't about how many copies you sell. You're not a book promoter. You want your book to promote YOU. It's what's known as your unique selling point (USP). Any business owner will tell you how important this is. It should be the foundation for anything you create.

Your perspective is what you have to offer. How many books are there on weight loss? This is because the same method doesn't work the same way for everyone. You may offer a unique perspective someone has been waiting for. Perhaps they can relate to you in a way they haven't been able to relate to others. This goes for any subject you're knowledgeable about.

Your book is about your message, your stories and your perceptions. People will connect with the way you communicate and want to be part of your community.

What if nobody reads it?

What if the people you're writing your book for just happened to read it, and it changed their life? This is a major reason for sending your work into the world. You may never meet or know that person whose life you changed, because you shared your experience.

Think of JK Rowling, the billionaire author of the *Harry Potter* series who got children all over the world to fall in love with reading again, because she had the courage to follow her passion for writing, despite the situation she was in at the time.

I'm not good at spelling and grammar

That's why the world is full of people who love this stuff. Knowing all of the rules surrounding grammar, and the intricacies that go with it, excites them. Your editor will know these rules, so you don't have to.

I'm not an expert. Who am I to write a book?

When I was putting together my first book on millionaires, I wanted to use a penname. I'm a female writing in what's considered a male-dominated field. Also, I was prominent in my chosen medical career, which had nothing to do with writing or millionaires. I didn't want to tell anyone about it, in case they laughed. To be honest, I was concerned what people would think of me.

Of course, I eventually decided to use my own name in order to establish myself in my capacity as an author. As I kept publishing books, my original fears fell away, and people respected me in my new role.

You don't have to be an expert. You can seek out authorities in their field to contribute to your book or as a co-author, thus making you the reporter or researcher. Investing your time and energy gathering the information will make you an expert.

Though I could provide more examples, I think you get the idea. It's not just about authoring a book. Excuses based in fear can extend to any area of your life. Maybe you don't want to rock the boat by asking for a pay raise or you think that person you're attracted to will turn you down if you ask for a date, so why bother? Perhaps you have had a fantastic business idea, but the thought of bringing it to fruition churns up all of your insecurities.

I've felt these fears and experience them all of the time. And guess what? So do all successful people. They just don't let it stop them. It doesn't go away. Successful people understand fear is good. It means they're stretching and growing.

I used to be fearful of horses, because I fell off one when I was a child. The universe delivered me a teacher in the form of my daughter, who absolutely loves horses and had a dream many little girls share: she wanted her own pony. In order to make this dream come true, I had to learn about horses. I read a bit, got a volunteer position at the Riding for the Disabled, attended several clinics and slowly but surely learnt to understand horses. Had I not taken action to overcome my fear, my daughter would not have realised her dream of the most beautiful black pony with a perfect white love heart marking on her forehead, aptly named Dream. Also, my family would not have experienced acreage living in our dream property. I even learnt to get back in the saddle.

Fear will absolutely be part of this journey, so make friends with it. It's there to protect you. When I walk onstage to do a presentation, all I focus on is serving the people who've taken time to be there to listen and learn. It's not about me but about helping and serving others. When you focus on helping someone else, the fear often disappears. Understand there's a much bigger force guiding you, so take the time to listen. You may discover you're in the flow, and before you know it you'll have words on the page.

Resistance will always be there on any path you take in this life, no matter what it is you set out to do. Recognise it as a little test. You're the author of your life, whether it's a blank page, a blank canvas or a music sheet, and you get to create it.

If someone tells me they can't write, I tell them the story of my daughter and how she wrote a book when she was eleven, because she didn't have the limiting belief that she couldn't. She authored her own children's book called *Pandora and the Perfect Egg*. What I love most about this is how she didn't know children don't usually write children's books. When I tell clients about it, they share what they've learnt in order to help other children publish their own books.

Pandora and the Perfect Egg is available in print and e-book everywhere and has also been donated and distributed to Books for PNG kids, The Gold Coast University Hospital children's ward as part of their get-well bags, The Smith Family, The Royal Children's Hospital Brisbane, Balinese children and the Sunrise of Africa School in Kenya.

Seeing children's faces light up while repeating the lines and recognising how producing a book can give so much joy to others, is beyond words.

Remember, courage isn't the lack of fear. It's having the fear and taking action anyway.

▶ Action

When taking action in any area of your life, there's one important idea to keep in mind:

Go with your gut

If it feels right, then you need to take inspired action and trust your instincts when you're offered an opportunity. Pay attention to that little voice in your head that whispers to you. This is what successful people do. This whisper is what inspired me to author a book.

▶ Mentor

Most successful people had a mentor, someone who championed their journey and showed them the ropes. Mentors are the fastest way to your outcome and will save you years of toiling and making mistakes. They fast track your success.

▶ Model

You have two models to choose from:

1. The *Hope and Pray* method with a twist of DIY.

2. Investing in education in order to save yourself time and money by following a proven model.

Which model sounds better to you?

▶ Invest

Successful people invest in themselves, their education and their product. They also engage professionals. If you focus on what you're passionate about and find someone else who's passionate about those areas where you're not as proficient, you've created a match made in heaven. Isn't success about loving what you do? My editor loves to edit, and she's a success. My beauty therapist is amazing at what she does, and I love spending time with her for a massage or facial, because she oozes gratitude and happiness, and I get the reward of feeling that love radiated to me.

▶ Share

Successful people love to share what they know with others. They share their expertise, knowledge and experience through their books, blogs, programs, workshops, seminars and webinars. It brings me great joy knowing you're reading this now and understanding why I love books and am passionate about fast-tracking the success of authors who share their passion with the world.

➤ Help

Successful people are fulfilled when they help others achieve their level of success while getting to witness the transformation.

What I know is that every one of you has a book inside of you, and by making it real you will benefit financially, spiritually, emotionally, personally and professionally.

My authors are often surprised when I tell them the planning phase is the most important part of the process, but once they get involved in it, they tell me nothing else ever gave them such clarity around their business, product or service. This is because when creating a book, it's essential to order and organise your knowledge.

This is what most people don't do. Money flows where information is the most ordered and organised, and this is why authors can expect to be paid higher fees, are offered more speaking opportunities, are recognised by the media as the expert and have clients coming to them. Simply put, you become the *author-ity*. By this I don't mean you have a huge ego and think you're better than anyone else. I prefer to think of *author-ities* as people who are passionate and authentic. Positioning and credibility are part of the territory when becoming a published author. The doors start to open, and the opportunities flow. Here's the main point I want to get across: you have to publish your book to reap these rewards and fast track your success.

The Book Diet

Consuming a lot of books in any format is a great way for you to prepare to write your own. It's almost like osmosis. You get a feel for the author's style, which should give you an idea as to helpful information you could impart to help others. Also take a look at the covers that catch your eye and you feel best represents the material, so when it comes time to choose your own cover, you'll be more focused. Remember: a book isn't about you. It's about sharing what you know, so you can help others.

My main purpose for creating this book at this time is that it enables me to leverage my time. Instead of having a lot of conversations about what I do, I can now direct someone to my book and maybe inspire them to self-publish or become part of the *Author Express* or *Author-ity* program, so I can have the privilege of guiding them on their journey.

The library is full of *free* wisdom. There are applications (apps) that deliver e-books and audiobooks directly to your devices, without you ever leaving your home. All you need is a library card.

You might want to inform your friends and family about your plans to write a book. For instance, when people announce they're going on a diet, they'll feel more compelled to stay on it when going into situations where they might be tempted to cheat. Not only that, but once you've made the decision to eat healthier, you come up with a plan to make it easier on yourself. You make sure the right foods are in your fridge and plan your exercise schedule. Perhaps to keep you motivated, you can get a workout or walking buddy. By surrounding yourself with health and making those around you involved in the process, you'll be much more motivated.

Creating your book is no different. You need to prepare your writing environment and schedule time to consistently work on it. You may have to cancel TV watching or change your schedule to fit in some writing time. Perhaps you know the perfect environment where you won't be disturbed, should you choose to dictate your book. I've even heard of people using their walk- in- wardrobe and an ironing board as a makeshift desk, just to get a quiet space for a while, away from the household happenings. Don't let this be your excuse. It's a good idea to make your writing space a location you walk by frequently, so you'll feel inspired to sit down and tap out a few words.

Your Book is a Business Card and Brochure for Your Business

The first time I ever heard someone say your book is a business card on steroids, I was hooked. At the time, not only didn't I have a business, I didn't want to become a published author. This made me an anomaly, and publishing was more difficult to accomplish than it is now.

The results of a *New York Times* survey were that eighty-one percent of adults wanted to be a published author. In my experience, I've discovered there are three main reasons most people want to write a book;

1. Share a message

A lot of people want to share a message or write a memoir about their life. This is an amazing legacy to leave in the world and may be your passion story. A legacy is what you leave behind and are remembered by. Your book can remind others what goals you've achieved and where you failed or succeeded.

By painting vivid pictures with your stories, you can bring people into your world and make them feel as if they're experiencing it for themselves.

But please remember that people often relate more to adversity. By meeting them where they are, you're able to form a deeper bond with your reader. If they're picking up your book to pull them out of a slump, the last thing they want to read about is how successful and wealthy you are, without hearing the struggles that came beforehand.

If you share your story of adversity, people aren't going to think less of you. They'll relate better and learn more. They'll have hope there's an end in sight, since you've been through the same circumstances and triumphed over your situation.

The subject of your book might be the reason you started your business. Maybe you've experienced a tragedy, and writing a book is a way to deal with your feelings and be at peace. Or you set what seemed to be an impossible goal and accomplished it. For example, doctors may have said you'd never walk again, and you wound up climbing a mountain. Always keep in mind that your story is unique, and you may connect with someone and help them turn their life around.

The world needs your message and expertise, and a book allows you to share it. The good news is that you can make money and make a difference at the same time.

Those who've written books are ordinary people like you, they just had the courage to write down what they know and share their message and experiences. In other words, they've organised their material and put their thoughts on paper. It's that simple.

So often I hear, "I just want to make a difference and help people." That's great, but what I've learnt in the years since starting my book series is that you need to make money at the same time. By adding your book as a marketing tool, you promote yourself and your expertise.

If you're savvy and plan from the start what to include that could help the reader and make your book more readable, then you're going to have a much better chance of your book being a success.

Mark Victor Hanson, of the *Chicken Soup For the Soul* book series, said, "A book can really *pedestalise* you." In other words, it puts you on this pedestal to help you stand out from the crowd, so you're seen as the *author-ity*. It's a powerful thought to have as you tell your story. But for now, just enjoy the process. All you need to concentrate on is spreading your message, adding value to people's lives, and becoming the *author-ity* in your niche.

The reason for writing a book is going to be different for everybody. You might want to brand your business, share a life lesson or leave a legacy. It could even be a combination of all three.

2. Money

People think they want money, but really, they want what money can give them. It's only when you pursue your goals with passion that your dreams can thrive. This is a healthy way to live your life, as opposed to being in constant pursuit of money.

Your book needs to be about a subject you love. You're going to put a lot of time and energy into creating it. Once it's out in the world, it becomes your marketing asset for the next five years, so be prepared to live and breathe it. If you're not in love with your chosen topic, then you're going to have a difficult time staying focussed.

There are a lot of people who've made money by finding a gap in the market and publishing a book on the subject to fill it. While this approach is entrepreneurial, it's also the path to writing ninety-nine cent e-books on topics you're not passionate about, just to earn a dollar. The best kind of success is doing what you love.

I encourage my authors to think outside of the box. Your book is meant to promote you, not to make you become a writer or a book promoter. Selling twenty-dollar paperback books is also not the path to riches. About one in twelve-million books goes on to sell over a million copies. I call this the hope-and-pray method. As the icing on the cake it's great, but there are much better ways to make money from your book than selling it. Remember, it's about the business behind the book where the real wealth is. The book gives you credibility, and then the products and services behind the business is where the money is.

There are many more opportunities that come to published authors, so what's the cost to you in lost opportunity by not being published?

Successful marketers give away free copies of their book when they launch. This is because the lifetime value of a customer is more important to them than the money from actual book sales.

3. Marketing

This is the sweet spot me. At the point you can share your message, make money and create a marketing asset is when your book becomes your best friend, your PR person and your 24/7 sales team.

It starts with knowing what your book is a calling card for. It may be a seminar, workshop, retreat, lead generator or client gift. This is the part where you think about the business behind it.

If you love to cook or bake, your book becomes the brochure for your classes. If you're a healer, it becomes the brochure for the retreats you run. Get the picture? You don't need to have the backend business set up yet, but you do need to start with the end in mind if you want your book to be more than sharing your message.

Unlike with a business card, people don't throw your book away. Instead, it goes on their desk or into their bookshelf or nightstand. They share it with friends and relatives. There are books I've read years after receiving them and passed them on to a friend.

When you see the big picture, you'll change your mindset around gifting them. After all, you can produce a bookstore-quality book for less than the price of a good gift card and definitely less than that bottle of wine you send to a client for the holidays.

Another great asset to writing a book is that it can be a hugely successful way of raising awareness about a charity. John Wood, who wrote the book *Leaving Microsoft to Change the World*, tells the story about how he quit Microsoft because he was unfulfilled. He went on to set up a children's charity where they build libraries in Third-World countries and get people to donate books.

Author Action Steps

→ Figure out your topic.

→ State the outcome you hope to achieve.

→ Jot down your vision for the business behind your book.

→ Come up with some working titles and subtitles.

STEP TWO: PRODUCE

"Writing a non-fiction book is simply a matter of organising and ordering your knowledge."

When you think about your book as organising and ordering your knowledge, it takes all of the mystery away and puts you in the correct head space.

It doesn't take years to write a book. This is a common misconception. You just need to have the courage to write down what you know in a clear and concise manner.

Think Skinny!

Gone are the days when you had to write down everything you know on a subject. You've probably led an interesting life and as a result have more than one book in you.

I will often suggest to my authors that they write a skinny series of books or a standalone skinny book. You don't need to pen *War and Peace*. Your reader doesn't want an encyclopaedia. We're in the knowledge age. They want to receive the information in a nice, condensed fashion, so they can digest and implement it right away. Because it's so lightweight, you can mail your book to potential clients as a way to start a conversation and leverage your time.

I've found this method invaluable. Besides using my book to help clients get the big picture of the steps and strategies needed to write their own, I also wanted to be able to give copies to people who attend my seminars or are interested about strategic partnerships and becoming part of my author programs.

One of my authors wrote a book for busy property managers and is now writing a skinny series, with each book relating to a specific day of her workshop across five topics. We already know her target audience is mostly women, as they are her existing clients. This meant producing a book that was small enough to fit inside a handbag, while also having enough information to make it interesting yet consumed in a short amount of time, and inexpensive enough to post bulk copies. Not only that, we wanted to include a free audio version property managers could listen to as they drove around inspecting properties.

All of this was planned from the start, so we could then reverse engineer the process and work back to how many words were needed and design everything around a smaller book.

Initially, she was going to have one manuscript with all five topics, but breaking it up means she can have a series of fresh content while giving her traction in her business. She could begin marketing the seminar relating to that book, get some skin in the game and have the next four books and seminars already in the hopper.

What I love about this author is that she wrote the book in thirty-minute increments every morning while still in bed, and in a matter of months she had a quality published book in the hands of a thousand current and potential clients.

She was invited to be interviewed on a radio show she'd wanted to guest on for over six years and became a keynote speaker in her industry. Did she know all of this would happen at the start? No, but she planned for it and published with purpose.

What Type of Book Should You Write?

Knowing the reason you're authoring a book will determine the type of book you write. Each has a specific purpose if you include the right information. The four main types of books I suggest for business owners are:

1. Core Idea Book: aka, The Expert IP Book

   This is a book based on your knowledge and expertise (your IP) in the area you work in or want to work in. The book will be from your personal point of view and should only be published if you intend to remain in this occupation for a minimum of three to five years. It's a great way to save time by sharing your core ideas with clients before meeting with them, so they can know if they're a good fit for your methods.

This is an example of a core idea book. Other examples include relationship advice and property development and management. Basically anything that signifies a niche knowledge is a core idea book.

Most of my authors produce this style of book.

2. Creative Book: aka, The Coffee Table Book

This is for people whose work is reflected through pictures as opposed to words. For example, this style would be good for landscape designers, architects, artists and photographers. They can be slightly more expensive to produce, particularly in colour, but the advantage is that they can be put on display in office reception rooms to showcase your work. One of my current authors is using this method to display her gorgeous opal jewellery and showcase her stones. A children's book can also fall under this category.

3. Compiled book: aka, The Lazy Author Book

This may be a collection of interviews, case studies, stories, tips or as simple as a collection of quotes. I refer to this style lovingly as *The Lazy Author Method*. Coaches would benefit from this type of book, as they may have a collection of tips or daily inspirational quotes that will get the reader thinking of you each morning.

It can also be collection of interviews, which is the method I used to produce my *Millionaire* book series and publish the *Elevate* book series. Authors in my programs use this method to become published authors by collaborating with others and using their content.

4. Concept book: aka, The Allegory Book

This is where the author takes a key concept or message and turns it into an allegory to get their message across. An example would be *Who Moved my Cheese* in which four characters represent people's reaction to change. You can also use a combination of fiction and non-fiction in the same book. An example of this would be *The One Minute Millionaire* by Mark Victor Hanson, in which the left side of the book gives advice, while the right side illustrates the point with fictionalised dramas. Robin Sharma has also used this method to great effect.

Though this may sound intriguing and interesting, you probably shouldn't choose this method unless you're already an experienced writer. Taking your knowledge and turning it into a simple, engaging story that correctly illustrates your point isn't as easy as it looks. If you're in the self-help field and have some writing experience under your belt or want to test your method in writing classes, then this is a great way to connect with your readers.

How Long Should My Book Be?

I'm always asked by clients how long their book should be, and I always answer with my own question: "How many words will it take to get your point across?" If your words aren't impactful and are just padding to make your book a certain length, then you'll lose your readers. They're only interested in gaining knowledge, so the word count isn't really of interest to them. Getting your point across in a clear, concise manner should be your ultimate goal.

Here is a guide to the word counts for the different types of books:

▸ Skinny Book (part of a series): 15-20,000 words
▸ Skinny Book (standalone): 25-35,000 words
▸ Standard Book: 35-50,000 words
▸ Compilation Book: 50-80,000 words

In terms of the physical size of your book, the way in which it's formatted, designed and typeset comes into play, as well as the font size and the amount of tables, diagrams, quotes and white space utilised. As an example, this book is around 30,000 words.

The size of your manuscript should be designed with your target audience in mind. Will they have it on their desk as a reference book or carry it in their handbag or briefcase? Will you sell it at a seminar or use it as a gift or giveaway? Will you have to post it?

If you intend to mail a lot of copies, you might want to keep it skinny to reduce postage costs. In Australia, the letter post sizes are up to 1kg, with the next step up being 3kg and includes an enormous price increase. The cost could get prohibitive if you're not charging for the book, so there are a lot of factors to keep in mind. If it's going to be spine-out on a bookstore shelf, you'll want a standard format with a spine thickness large enough for the title to stand out.

If it's going to be sold online in any format, the front cover is the most important element. Your best bet is to format the cover for a thumbnail. Often it means optimising your print book cover. If you hire a good book designer, you won't have to worry.

Getting the Words Out of Your Head and Onto the Page

This is all about getting what's between your ears and turning it into a manuscript. If the thought of sitting and writing your book stops you in your tracks, then don't worry. There are other ways.

This could simplify and demystify the process for you:
Every book you've ever read is a combination of twenty-six letters.

To go from idea to the page, I suggest you use a simple three-step system.

1. Book Brainstorm

I've been told that writing a book is like vomiting up all of the words before organising where they go. You can do this alone or with someone who knows your content well. The method I use with my authors is to ask them questions that lead to more and more ideas. This isn't about getting it right or keeping it in any order. It's just a brain dump. Most authors get inspired, because it gets the creative juices flowing.

One idea is to get a big piece of butcher paper, a whiteboard or chalkboard and let the ideas flow.

2. Book Board

This is where your ideas start to take shape. There are a few ways you can do this. One method is to use mind mapping. There are a plethora of free online tools to help you create a mind map, and I can tell you from experience it works, as it's how I broke publishing a book down into five simple steps.

If you're feeling overwhelmed by the process, this is a great way get your ideas ordered and organised, so you can see it all come together. Use sticky notes, and affix the main ideas to a wall, fridge or whiteboard to start sorting out what will go where.

These methods allow your book to be fluid, which means you can continue to play with the order. This is an exciting stage, because you start to think of more and more information you can include as you shuffle the sticky notes around and add more ideas.

3. Book Map

This is where your book takes on a structure and a framework. You basically transform your brainstorm and board into a one-page document that becomes your book blueprint.

You know what your table of contents looks like, what case studies you'll include, what your steps are and possibly even have a working title. Your book map and subtitle can keep you focussed on what information you want to share, or even if you want to make it into a series.

These steps don't have to take long and can be lots of fun. You'll discover it's a simple strategy to get your knowledge out of your head, so it makes sense to the reader. It saves so much time down the track and will prevent writer's block, because you already know what you're going to put where.

Writing Your Book

There are a few ways you can produce a book that depend on your publishing outcome. Whether you're great at typing or not, there's a method for you.

1. Write It

Again, meet people where they are in order to communicate effectively with them. They're looking for a cure or a solution. It's so important to be human and relatable by starting your story from when you were struggling and not by bragging about how big your house is or how many cars you have.

The best style or tone for your book is to write as if you're having a conversation with your reader. With a structure or a framework, you'll be able to get everything out of your head and your heart. When you know the shape your book is going to take, it's much easier for the words to flow.

When creating your first draft, just write. Don't stop to correct typos and sentence structure. Just let your brain create the content. Do you think you don't have time? Try waking up thirty minutes earlier. You'll be surprised what you can accomplish in a short amount of time if you did the previous steps correctly.

You need to shut down all distractions. Your only thought should be how your advice can make the reader's dream a reality. Turn off your phone, social media and all email pop ups. That way you'll be totally focussed, and the words will just flow. Every now and then you'll need to go for a walk or do some form of exercise. Not only will it prevent burnout, but it could also be the catalyst for more ideas to help the reader on their journey.

In my *Author Express* program, I go much more in depth and have templates and blueprints to assist authors in developing a structure. My clients tell me they help with confusion and roadblocks.

For instance, *The Book Blueprint* is a fantastic tool that can help you get your book finished in a matter of days. The program includes video demonstrations for each step along the way, templates for identifying your audience and how to position your book to act as your 24/7 sales team.

Authors in my program, who in the beginning said there was no way they could write a book, have surprised themselves and grew to love the process. When you sort out your thoughts and get clarity, it will reinspire you in your own business, such as seeing a gap where there's the potential for a whole new product line or service you could provide.

The *Author Express* program was developed, because people would always ask me how they could publish a book. It took off from the start. The process of putting it together was basically the same as creating this book, except that I recorded video presentations of my content.

In fact, the book came after the program. This is because I wanted a business card to take to my speaking events and use in joint-venture relationships. I also wanted to run my pilot program and have people successfully finish it before having it actively marketed. The program took me six months to put together. I published each video as I went, because I'm visual, and it helped me to understand where I was and what else I needed to add.

2. Talk your book

This method is great for those who say they don't have time to write a book but love to talk. Or maybe you only know the hunt and peck method of typing. As the prolific author, Seth Godin says, "No one ever gets *talker's* block."

A great method to get your ideas in order is to have someone interview you and keep you on track, so you don't ramble. Your interviewer can be someone you know or hire. Experienced interviewers are used to cutting through all of the red tape and getting to the heart of the question. Alternatively, you could use your book map to record yourself. There are many apps to choose from that turn your voice into text, and most of the time you can record directly into your smartphone.

Google Doc's voice-typing feature is great. Just speak into your computer microphone, and the words appear on the page. As technology is constantly on the move, you could search for other ways to talk your book that suits your style and device.

Another great way is to host a webinar series and have it turned into a book or audio. You can run it over a ten-week period, and bingo, you have your chapters.

These methods allow you to write in conversational English that makes the book easy to read. Keep it simple and deliver your message clearly, so your reader will receive it and tell others about you.

If you talk faster than you write, this would be a great method for you.

3. Ghost Writer or Ghost Author

This method is great for those who have great ideas and information but find it difficult to organise it all and put it into a book.

A ghost writer, or as I like to call them, ghost author, is someone who writes your book for you in your voice. Most celebrities, icons and politicians use this method. They pay someone a fee to write their story for them. This strategy makes sense if you feel your time is better spent on doing what you love.

Even within the ghost writing/authoring methods, you have some options. If you regularly speak at events and conferences and record them, you can get transcripts and give them to a writer to organise and make it cohesive. Another method is for the writer to interview you to gain an understanding of your expertise.

This can be expensive, but technology and outsourcing can make this option more viable than in the past. One platform where you can find these freelance services is Upwork.

4. Compile Your Book

This method is for those who want to start a niche business but may not be an expert in the field or don't have enough content and want to grow a brand using other people's content (OPC). As the author, you're responsible for compiling all of the information to form the manuscript and publish it. A great benefit to this method is that you get to meet and associate with leaders in your industry, and even become friends with them. Also, it's a fantastic way to position yourself in your industry by association.

This method has been my secret weapon. It's collaborative and a win-win. The idea here is to have all contributors add knowledge in the form of content that you compile and publish. Multiple contributors can add a few pages or a chapter, and the end result is a book.

When I put together my *Property Millionaire* book, although I'd done a lot of renovating and even a small development, I wasn't an expert, so I found a co-author who had a lot of property contacts in the area. We invited all of the experts in their niche to contribute a chapter, thus making the book a comprehensive overview of the ways they made money from property.

At the time I was compiling the book, I was also involved in overseeing a development project, so I had the advantage of having many experts' advice at my fingertips I could call and ask for advice. In the beginning, I didn't know many of the contributors, but by the end they became lifelong friends. Once the book was completed and published, the contributors were able to use it to showcase their niche and the programs or services they offered, as well as mentor others to do the same.

And because they all contributed financially, the project paid for itself.

I've taught this method to my authors who are using them to produce and publish their books. Those who choose to engage my *Author Express* program learn how to monetise and pre-sell thousands of copies prior to printing.

If you think people can't be successful with this method, consider *The Secret*, which consisted of interviews with experts about the law of attraction that was extracted from the movie and hugely popular *Chicken Soup for the Soul* book series. The authors compiled 101 stories from the many sent in to them, and they never had to write a word.

Another option is to put together a book of quotes, tips or hacks in relation to your industry.

Perfectionism and Polishing

What I love about being an author is that you don't need a PhD in writing or literature to be a best-seller. The term is best-*selling*, not best writing. I'm sure you've heard of books that shot to fame because they were well marketed, and a lot of hype was generated, even though a lot of criticism surrounded the actual writing.

Most manuscripts never see the light of day, as the writer procrastinates and keeps reading and editing it in an effort to make it perfect. Though it's important to make sure your book is of good quality and contains useful information, waiting for it to be perfect can keep you in limbo. There are online print-on-demand companies that allow you to print one copy at a time, so it's easy to make changes between versions and can be a great way to add to or update your content.

To be clear, I'm not advocating that you produce a non-professional book. In fact, I want you to put your best work out there. A good editor can help take your rough draft and turn it into a work of art, because they love what they do and are passionate about helping you bring your message to the world in the best possible way. Don't let perfectionism stop you.

Editing is not negotiable. I love editors, because they make us non-writers sound fantastic. As one of my clients said, "They took me from track pants and turned me into Chanel." Even the best writers in the world use an editor to make sure everything flows and makes sense.

There are many different levels of editing, and the type you choose depends on your style of book and the shape of the raw manuscript. Sometimes they will need to move content around in order to make it flow better. All good editors will take out extraneous words and leave your core message intact and reader-friendly, while keeping it in your voice.

Proofreading is the final check for spelling and grammar. Though you may want to rely on the editor to do the proofreading, it's not a good choice. They have read your manuscript too many times and may see words and punctuation that aren't there or are misused. Different functions use different parts of the brain. You need a fresh set of eyes and someone who's trained to spot these small errors.

Again, it's imperative you not skip this step, unless you want bad book reviews. Remember: presenting a professional book to the world is a reflection of you and your brand. Readers are smart and can tell instantly when someone hasn't used a professional editor and designer, and it's a big turn-off.

Optional Content

▶ Testimonials

Testimonials can be invaluable when someone considers buying or reading your book and can also give them a rough idea of how it might benefit them, especially if the testimonial speaks to them in terms of commonality. For instance, the reader might be in the same place as the person giving the testimonial, and if they discover that person is now a huge success, they'll want to find out more. Talk to your clients or customers and let them know early on you'd like a testimonial. A good method is to put them on the back cover, where they're easy to find, or in the first few pages of the book.

▶ Foreword

A foreword is generally written by someone with credibility or recognition in your field. I talk to authors who are unwilling to approach someone they consider an authority, which is ironic, because they're publishing a book that makes them the *author-ity*.

More often than not, the person is more than happy to be invited. Getting an endorsement from a respected expert in your field can add credibility to you, and your book by association. Often they will want to see the cover and the contents before they agree, especially if you add their name to the cover.

One word of warning. While your confidence will increase due to writing a book, you need to understand that Bill Gates and Oprah probably aren't going to be chomping at the bit to write your foreword, so aim for someone who has clout in your industry you can realistically approach. You can still aim high. Just make sure you have the right approach and contacts. For instance, I've been able to secure forewords from Dr John

Gray. Author of *Men are from Mars, Women are from Venus* and Dr John Demartini from *The Secret*.

While a foreword can be a great addition to your book, it's not mandatory, so if you don't have the right contacts yet, don't worry about it. My program will assist you with this step.

▶ Dedication and acknowledgements

This is where you get to credit those that have assisted you on your journey. The book can be dedicated to anyone you wish, from family, to community, to a mentor or perhaps someone you haven't met, like potential clients or prominent experts in your field who inspire you.

▶ Disclaimer page

The disclaimer page appears at the front of the book and includes all of the publishing information, ISBN and copyright details.

Disclaimers can vary depending on the style of book you're writing. A memoir should contain a statement that some names and details may have been changed to protect the privacy of individuals. A fiction book will often state that all characters are fictitious, and any resemblance to real-life events or persons is coincidental. A how-to advice book would usually state that the advice is general in nature, the opinions are the author's, and individuals may need to seek professional advice.

▸ **Introduction**

A great introduction by the author can set the scene and let the reader know what they can expect. It can also cover how the book is organised and the concepts covered.

▸ **Conclusion**

The conclusion may contain a brief summary overview and/or the next steps the reader should take on their information journey.

▸ **ISBN, barcode library registrations**

These are the bits and pieces that make your book professional and available throughout the world for distribution. If you intend only to sell copies in the back of the room at your seminars, you may not require an ISBN. However, for that professional look I would recommend it. You never know where the book could end up, and though not impossible, it's difficult to go back and add it at a later date.

An ISBN is like a thumbprint. It's unique to all formats of your book and the easiest way to remember it. Each version of your book, such as audio, paperback, hardcover and e-book, requires its own ISBN, so each person knows the exact version they're purchasing.

If you follow the book blueprint, you'll know which pages to put where and how to get a foreword from industry experts. You'll also get testimonial and disclaimer examples, as well as videos that demonstrate how to get all of the legal bits and pieces that will make your book official.

▶ The Extras

You can add nice touches in your book that will keep the reader engaged and cement what they've learned. There are so many options to include that will make it more engaging and reader-friendly. It all depends on the topic and type of book you're writing. Examples may include cartoons, diagrams, tables, case studies, images and success stories, both yours and your clients/customers.

People learn through story, and there's a way to make it extra memorable. If you're creating your book as a business card, it's important to include a call to action, so the reader can continue working with you long after reading it. A call to action can be directing the reader to your website or blog, an offering or giveaway such as a free session, providing them with an advanced chapter of your next book or a discount on one of your seminars.

Get people excited about what you're offering, so they tell all of their friends and relatives about it. Word of mouth will help spread your message.

Author Action Steps

➜ Have a book brainstorm to get the creative juices flowing and put your ideas in order.

➜ Determine what type of book you want to write.

➜ Determine a method for producing your book.

➜ Decide on your dedication.

➜ Choose who you'd like to approach to write the foreword.

STEP THREE: PACKAGE

"Packaging your book is all about attracting and communicating the book's outcome with your audience"

I always tell my authors their book has a face, a voice, a spine and insides, and they need to understand its anatomy and psychology in order for it to be successful. First impressions absolutely count. Your book is an extension of you and your brand. This is the point when you package your manuscript and make it into a book. The process will vary slightly depending on whether you intend to publish a print book, e-book or both.

Designing your book's cover and inside pages and watching it all come to life is exciting. There are two parts to your packaging your book's content:

The Exterior Cover

Here's the information that should be considered for the outside of your book:

- title
- subtitle
- imagery
- author name
- author pic and bio
- testimonial
- colours
- fonts
- back cover copy
- barcode
- spine (often neglected and incorrect).

There's a little bit of psychology to a book's cover, and competent designers will know and understand this concept. As most authors self-publish these days, the author has the responsibility of ensuring their book cover attracts the right audience.

Now I'd like to discuss the cover, inside design and layout of your book, often referred to as typesetting.

▶ Outside Cover

We do judge a book by its cover. This is what sells books, because the reader has no idea of your content yet, so your cover must attract the right audience. It's a must in order to package your book professionally.

The cover is your book's first impression. It's what the book buyer/reader looks at before deciding whether they will turn it over and read the back or return it to the shelf. When people go your website and social media sites or browse online bookstores, your cover will be the most important element to pull them in.

While you may think your Photoshop skills are top notch, you should understand it's not only about making the picture look nice. Likewise, your local logo designer may be an expert at what they do, but this involves an entirely different set of skills.

What most first-time authors don't realise is that having a fantastic cover is the most important part of the book's marketing. You're creating an asset. Treat this aspect the same way you would hiring a professional to represent your business. Expert cover designers have an eye for detail and understand the elements of what makes a book cover great.

My books covers have been shown on national television, in magazines and newspapers. They appear in book distributors' brochures, on presale order forms and bookmarks, and are shown on presentation slides, social media posts and banners.

Once you start thinking about the numerous opportunities for your book to be seen, you'll understand how the simple act of creating a great cover generates leverage that can be used over and over.

Even individual elements can be used and branded across other marketing collateral, such as banners for your YouTube, Facebook and Twitter accounts. It can be resized for podcast art, pull-up banners and business cards. When someone types your name into Google, it will come up in their images.

My *Millionaire* books and *Millionaire School*® brands were all created using the same style of font and logo featured on the book cover. This means the online and offline brand was consistent and recognisable.

If you want someone to read your book, then your cover needs to spark their interest almost immediately, or they'll move on to the next one fairly quickly. The cover needs to tell the reader about quite a few elements in only a few seconds. It must "talk" to them in terms of:

▶ the book genre
▶ the book title
▶ the subtitle
▶ the author.

It should also portray what the book is about and if it will benefit the reader by giving them what they're looking for. To do this, the cover needs to have the right colours that evoke the required emotions and the typography and imagery that sends the right messages.

Old fonts can make the content seem outdated, particularly if it's a how-to book. The potential buyer will naturally presume the information is no longer viable and look for something more modern.

Let's say you have a book entitled *How to Be Happy*, but your cover colours are dark and dreary, and your images evoke sombreness. If a person is depressed, and your book only makes them feel worse, you've just spent a lot of time and energy on a book nobody will read.

▶ Title

While I always tell my authors to trust their instincts, I also tell them they need to do their research first. There are a number of different theories regarding titles.

Keyword rich

Some people suggest keyword-rich titles. This means choosing words that people would search for. As an example, if your book is about pregnancy, using that word in the title is good for search optimisation on Google and Amazon. However, I wouldn't suggest titling a book solely based on ranking or because someone thinks it's a good idea. It will all come back to your strategy.

Again, if you're selling your book at your speaking engagements, then you have more flexibility. What you need to be concerned about is that your title isn't confusing, because a confused mind will reject the information being offered. Keeping it simple is a more effective way to reach your ideal reader.

Made-up word

Titles can be a made-up word, but it can work against you if people don't know what your book is about. If you decide to go with this method, a good subtitle can alleviate any confusion.

Twist on a well-known title

Some authors take classic self-help books such as *Think and Grow Rich* and *The 7 Habits of Highly Effective People* and make a word change to give it a slight twist. The new book might become *Speak and Grow Rich* or *The 7 Habits of Highly Effective Accountants*. Although this is allowed, it's been overdone. You want a title that reflects your authentic self. Your potential reader may think you can't come up with any unique ideas and are only copying from others.

An even more extreme version of this is using the same, or similar, title as a successful book, since titles generally can't be copyrighted unless it's a trademarked series. But again, think about gaining the reader's respect. Do you want their first impression of you to be that you couldn't even come up with an original title for your book?

Twist on a well-known quote
Using a well-known quote such as *Happy Wife, Happy Life* can be manipulated to fit your title, and it has the added benefit of being instantly recognisable. Just like with similar book titles, you could put your own spin on it, such as, *Happy Lawyer, Happy Life*, which author and lawyer Clarissa Rayward recently titled her book.

This takes a little more ingenuity and also isn't associated with another book or author.

▶ Subtitle

In a nonfiction book, the subtitle can just be as powerful as the title and turn your book browser into a book buyer. When a potential reader picks up a book that's designed to help them, they want to know what's in it for them. Will it answer their questions? Your subtitle will clarify the message of your book.

The big error people make is attempting to craft a subtitle that's too general, in order to get more readers. If you're writing a core idea book and being positioned as an expert, it's a much better choice to be *niched*.

Sometimes a subtitle can leave the reader confused as to what the book is about. Maybe it's because the author tries to be interesting and clever, but making a person stand around trying to decipher your message is the fastest way to have them put your book back on the shelf and move on to the next. In this fast-paced age, people have a short attention span. If you don't grab them within the first few seconds, you've lost them.

▶ Imagery and colours

Colours evoke emotions, so it's important to choose wisely. If your book is about lifting people's spirits, then you want happy, bright colours. If you want to radiate feelings of wealth and success, you'll need to go with a completely different colour scheme.

Imagery is another powerful tool and is a quick way to get the reader to empathise with you. For instance, a book written by a military person who lost their leg can have their image on the front cover with their prosthetic limb. It sends a powerful message and is a fantastic way to fast track your connection to your potential reader. If you combine a great image and a great title, you have a guaranteed recipe for success.

▶ Fonts

You must use a font that represents the message you're trying to convey and the reader you're aiming to attract.

Using fonts that are difficult to read isn't a good choice. Remember, in the electronic versions of your book the first impression people will get of your cover will be a thumbnail image. If your title, subtitle and name all have different font styles, it can look too busy.

And again, if you believe you have the Photoshop skills to handle this, you should rethink it. While homemade is good for cookie recipes, your book having that appearance can make you seem unprofessional. People are looking for someone who takes pride in their work and will give them top-notch service. This method will tell them the opposite. Likewise, using an unprofessional template will just make your book blend in with everyone else's and won't help accentuate your uniqueness.

Having said this, I want to stress that it's okay to use templates if your budget doesn't stretch to cover the cost of a professional designer. Just do thorough research on covers that will sell and position your book. A striking image design can do wonders. Maybe you know an amateur photographer or can find someone just starting out who will charge a reasonable fee.

If you're under a crushing deadline, you can look into designers who offer premade covers that just need you to insert your name and book title. The difference is that they only use it once and don't rely on stock imagery.

Using a professional book designer means you don't need to understand the nitty gritty of design, though you should do research on what makes a cover great, because it will help when you send them your book cover brief. My goal in stressing the elements of design is to give you a better understanding of why it's best left to the professionals.

▶ Back Cover Copy

In the self-publishing market, the back cover usually suffers the most. The cover copy is your 24/7 sales team. If it's poorly designed, not legible and uses copious amounts of rambling words, nobody's going to pick it up, let alone want to read the words inside you've poured your blood, sweat and tears into.

You need to be clear and concise and speak to the reader by meeting them where they are. This way they'll know you understand them and have the answer for what they're looking for.

It's been said this part of the book can take longer to write than the rest. I'm not sure about that. If you know your readers and have spent time putting yourself in their shoes, while making sure you address what they need to know about your area of expertise, then it should be a simple task to craft some powerful bullet points and a few sentences that get the reader to understand yours is the book they're looking for.

Again, this copy will be used for multiple platforms, as well as for promoting your events or even a book launch.

Rather than looking at it as book prose, instead treat it as sales copy to encourage your potential reader to make the purchase. For a non-fiction book you'll need a short, sharp author bio and not your full CV or history. It should include the main reasons you have the authority to write a book on the subject and why they should listen to you. Being passionate about your topic is a great way to reach your readers, since they want someone who loves what they do. They know they'll be getting the best of what you have to offer. The urge to ramble and try to get as much information as possible into the copy is a mistake many first-time authors make. Rest assured that your reader can still get this information in other areas of your book.

The back cover copy needs to be in your voice, so if you're a quiet, professional, don't have a loud back cover with over the top sales copy. Remember to meet them where they are and answer their burning questions or desires.

▶ Spine

Again, this is where hiring a professional book designer can make the difference. For instance, someone without much professional experience could position the spine upside down. It happens more often than you think. On a bookshelf, the spine may be the only part that attracts your reader, so you want it done right. I can tell you that my clients who have their books in physical stores appreciate how professional and eye-catching it is.

The title and author name is the minimum amount of information to incorporate. If your book is thicker, you can include the subtitle if it won't look too cluttered.

▶ Inside Book Cover

The inside cover is a book's prime real estate but rarely used, and it's a missed opportunity. Not all printers will allow for it, and again it will come back to the strategy and purpose for your book. Some of my authors who print a larger volume of copies will use the back cover to advertise other books they've written, as well as products, services, events or even a tasteful advertisement promoting a strategic alliance that pays for the cost of the book's production. The other option is to include an author bio page. This is your book, and there are no rules. But be careful. Blatant advertising is frowned upon by bookstores, and they may refuse to carry it.

The ones who won't provide this service are most print-on-demand (POD) services, because it's more of a custom print job.

Book design can be subjective. When crafting the cover for this book, I had several designs created and asked the members of my *Author Express* program to vote. This cover won by a landslide.

While personally I love all things rainbows and unicorns, these are not the imagery or colours that would portray my core message of becoming an authority and being known in your niche.

With that said, I'd like to go into more detail as to the reasons this book cover was chosen. Perhaps one of them is why you chose this book, whether your decision was a conscious one or not.

Title

The title of the book is keyword rich, as well as being a clever play on the word authority.

The word author, as used in the title, suggests the broad topic of authorship and brings to mind a mental picture of a book. I added the *i-t-y*, because I wanted to speak to my target audience of business owners who are authorities in their field.

Adding the dash turns it into a made-up word that includes the outcome achieved, in that you become the authority by being a published author.

In the event I turn this into a skinny series, I can easily use different incarnations of the title to reflect the same imagery and idea.

Subtitle

I wanted the subtitle as three main points rather than a lengthy sentence.

They also form the acronym PIE (Publish, Increase, Expand) so it's easy for me to remember when mentioning it from stage or in an interview. After speaking with many business owners throughout the years, I've come to understand that while they can see the value in a book providing them with credibility, which leads to being able to expand their business, the actual process of writing and publishing doesn't fill them with joy. For this reason I deliberately didn't use words like *write your book*.

The subtitle, *Publish your book* (the action), *Increase your credibility* (the benefit) *and Expand your business* (the result/outcome), clearly demonstrates what the book is about.

Imagery and Colours

Again, because the writing process can evoke negative images to my target audience of business owners, I didn't want imagery of any kind of writing implement. What needed to be demonstrated is the result of being an industry leader.

Author-ity is a book about positioning yourself above the rest and increasing your credibility by becoming a published author. It's about attracting attention in order to have people seek you out, because you're the person who wrote the book.

This cover stands out, because it's different and daring. Red is an authority/power colour. If I was on brand, I would have considered blue for the cover, which also works for business books.

The arrows represent magnetism, which means people are drawn to that one authority, in this case, me, which is why my name is under the title of the book and not at the bottom. They also imply a sense of direction for people, who would like to be guided by me.

Fonts

The use of modern fonts portrays that the content is cutting edge and up to date.

I hope this information has helped you understand some of the intricacies of cover design. Just know that not everyone will agree with your choice and will have their own opinion of what a successful book cover looks like. For this reason it's important to survey your intended audience and not the local soccer club, unless your book is about soccer, in order to achieve a more satisfactory survey result.

The Interior Pages

If you plan to print your book in paperback format, you'll need to have it typeset, since it's entirely different from e-book formatting.

This is the meat and bones of your book. It's everything between the front and back cover. Now that you've hooked the reader, you need to design your manuscript in such a way that keeps them engaged enough to complete the book and immediately tell family and friends about it.

The most important factor to consider is making it easy to read. If the information looks packed together with not enough white space, it can overwhelm the reader. Also, don't use your Word fonts as a template, since it will look different once it's formatted for a book.

All of my books are published using a professional designer, as I wanted to produce a high-quality product, build a brand and leave a legacy to be proud of. First-time, self-publishing authors often skip this crucial step, thinking they can save money by doing it themselves, but the differences will be obvious, especially if it's sitting next to a professionally typeset book.

Be sure to include the correct pagination (numbering), where new chapters should start, headers and footers and the use of design to ensure a professional result.

If you still don't feel you can afford a design specialist, then look into purchasing a professional template that will give your book the same look and feel as those being churned out by the big publishing houses.

But please don't rule out professional book designers, because you think you can't afford them. I've known many who have great packages available. All of my clients who've utilised them felt it was money well spent. If you're not under a deadline, save your money and do it right.

Author Action Steps

→ Write down some working titles and subtitles.

→ Come up with colours and an image you feel would best showcase your message.

→ Research book covers and figure out what you like and why.

STEP FOUR: PUBLISH

"In order to share your message, make a difference and leave a legacy, you need to publish."

Now is the time to share your message and make it available to the wider public. There are basically two ways to publish your book.

The Slow Way

In the past, you could spend years writing your manuscript without ever knowing if your book would even be published. You might get discouraged after one or two rejections, convinced you have no talent. But you must persevere. There are so many people who receive a hundred rejection letters and kept going, no matter what.

One of the best examples of this is Jack Canfield, who co-authored the *Chicken Soup for the Soul* series. He was rejected 144 times before finally getting a small publisher to agree to print 20,000 books. As you probably know, this book launched a worldwide phenomenon, selling over five-hundred-million books and became one of the biggest brands ever built from a book series.

Dr Wayne Dyer began his career as a best-selling author by buying the entire first printing of his book from his publisher.

You can decide to go with the usual method and get a traditional publishing deal with a publishing house that will edit and package your book for you. However, with no existing author platform, large database or social media following, this can be a tough road that takes years. Before investing in a new author, publishers want to know there's an already-established fanbase, readership or audience.

The Fast Way

The fast way is self-publishing your book. In effect, you become the author and the publisher. Technology has totally disrupted the publishing industry. In fact, you're often using the same printing and distribution platforms as the big publishers. When Amazon first launched, your only option was to go through a publishing house. Now, authors can upload their e-book directly to Amazon Kindle.

The days of your manuscript being rejected are over. You have the final say on every aspect of your book. These days, self-published authors who later get offered traditional publishing contracts often turn them down. Even when authors choose to engage our team at *Author Express* to do some of the publishing aspects, it's still considered self-publishing.

Robert Kiyosaki originally self-published a thousand copies of his book *Rich Dad Poor Dad*. Deepak Chopra and Louise Hay also got their start by self-publishing.

Publishing Formats

The publishing format you decide on will depend on your avatar or book's purpose, who you want your audience to be and how you'd like them to consume your knowledge. Logic would dictate that the more formats you choose, the wider the audience you'll reach.

▶ **e-book publishing**
To publish your e-book, you'll need to have your edited and proofread manuscript formatted for the platform in which you'll be publishing. Some of the common formats

are ePUB, which is the most universal file type, or MOBI, which is exclusively for the Amazon kindle.

You can publish either directly to online stores such as Amazon, or to a distributor that will allocate your e-book to most, or all, of the online stores for you. In general, these platforms are free, and you pay a percentage of your book sales for the privilege of using them.

The advantage of this method is that they already have your customers going to their site to look for a book on your topic. Often, they also suggest titles for buyers who purchased a similar book, which means great exposure. Imagine your book recommended to readers who purchased *Rich Dad Poor Dad*, for example, which I've seen happen with my *Millionaire* books.

▶ Hardcopy or Paperback Publishing

If part of your strategy is to have a print book, which I personally am a huge fan of, then you need to decide if you will use a traditional printer or Print on Demand (POD). You need to select your printer prior to your book going to design, as your book designer has to prepare your files according to printing guidelines.

Normally, what you need to provide are a cover file and an inside pages file. POD allows you to print a single copy of your book, and distributors can also print and send the book directly to the customer who orders it. This means you won't need storage space for thousands of copies.

If you're a first-time author, I strongly suggest doing a small print run to start, and that's only after you've printed just one copy and made sure there are no obvious mistakes.

With POD, you're often limited in regards to paper stock, binding type and cover materials, but the range is quite good.

Traditional printers offer a much larger range of binding styles, cover materials and paper stocks, which means you can basically have anything you want. The downside is that you have to print in larger volumes, but the price comes down substantially with the amount of books you order. This is only a viable option if you're printing at least a thousand books. I generally recommend this type of publishing if you have a distribution channel, such as if you're a speaker or have a built-in large audience.

▶ Audiobook

Once you've created your print book, you can always repurpose it and turn it into an audiobook for those who prefer listening to the content while driving. Technology is constantly changing, so I won't go into the technical details here. However, I do cover aspects of it in my *Author Express* program.

You can decide to read and record your book yourself, which some of my authors have done, particularly when they're building a personal brand. I think consistency is important, particularly if your readers will come to your seminars and see you on a YouTube video or a podcast. Your audiobook could form a connection with these people before they meet you.

Another option is to hire a narrator who can even publish your book for you. If you choose to go this route, make sure it's done in a voice style similar to yours. If you're a middle-aged female with a low-pitched voice, then choosing a male voice, a young woman with a high-pitched voice or someone with a different accent, may do damage to your personal brand.

These days, you can quickly and easily print your book at the touch of a button and have it delivered around the globe without even touching it. I've run a publishing business for over eight years with nothing but a laptop, a phone and an idea.

Like I keep saying, your book is an asset, and just as with any asset, you have to invest in it. While as a business owner you want to receive a satisfactory return on investment (ROI), understand that you can create it once and reap the reward for years. It's an ongoing marketing tool.

Much like renovating a house you intend to sell, you may get to the end of the process and feel you don't have the money or energy for all of the finishing touches that will connect people emotionally with your book. Remember: most people buy with emotion and justify with logic.

Don't get to the end and decide to just 'get it done' and present an unprofessional, potentially unfinished product to the market. You can produce a book on any budget.

F.A.S.T publishing system

The whole process can go smoothly if you use my F.A.S.T. publishing system:

▶ Faster

With the explosion of technology and the availability of self-publishing services, getting your book out there is now faster and easier than ever before. I encourage all of my authors to take the publishing process into their own hands.

Although there's a time and place for traditional publishers, their process takes a lot longer to get to market, if your manuscript makes it that far. There's been many a time where my authors have a sudden pending deadline, because they've been invited to speak or run an event, and they're forced to package up their book in a matter of weeks. In the past this would have been impossible. Now, it's easily achievable.

▶ **A**ffordable

For the price of a good gift card, you can have a printed book in a matter of days.

Unlike a bottle of wine or chocolates, your book isn't something a client consumes and throws away. It's memorable, more personal and adds a lot more value. One of my authors, who's also a speaker, posted a copy of his book as a gift to industry leaders and ended up getting paid speaking gigs out of it. This means he delivers his message to a new audience, which translates to even more people getting inspired. And he gets paid to do it.

▶ **S**kinny

By now you can probably tell I'm a fan of the *skinny* book, which is smaller, usually with a slim spine width and provides specific content.

From the author's perspective, they gain momentum and see result sooner. It's also a great way to launch and go to market quicker, without compromising on quality. The author immediately gains *author-ity* in their industry, which means they can start to leverage the book right away.

From the reader's perspective, they want the information they've come for, and they're not concerned with how many words are included, as long as it answers their questions and provides the pertinent information. People love the sense of achievement when they've finished a book and are more likely to tell others about it.

This method also makes it easier to take some copies with you when you travel.

▶ Transportable

Gone are the days of posting off your books. I have some authors who travel and work all over the world, so this would be impossible for them. Your book can be downloaded to someone's device as a digital or audiobook in no time at all.

If you want to run a workshop in another city or country, your books can be printed and shipped to wherever you are. Recently, one of my authors was running a retreat in New South Wales and then doing a tour in Victoria. We ordered and shipped the books to each location ahead of time.

Author Action Steps

→ Consider in what format you'd like your book. Take into account your ideal client and their needs as you make your decision.

STEP FIVE: PROMOTE

"Promotion is about illuminating your message to improve the lives of others."

Most authors think that once their book is written their job is done, but the book is not the end, it's just the beginning. You can build your business by marketing and distributing your book. Start with friends and family. Email your community and use speaking opportunities to get the word out. Promotion is one of the most important steps in the process.

There are a myriad of ways to promote your book, and one of the best times to do it is before it's published. Start touting yourself as *The upcoming author of (insert name of your book)*. When you get to the design phase for your cover, post on Facebook and social media that you'd like opinions and start building a buzz.

Remember that the purpose of your book is to promote you and open doors, so be strategic about where and when you campaign, because you don't want to become a fulltime book seller. As I said, this isn't where the money is. You don't have to sell lots of books to be successful.

There are three main ways to promote your book and yourself as the *author-ity*.

1. Traditional Media

Traditional Media includes newspapers, magazines and radio and television appearances. As a general rule, they will occur as a result of submitting a media release to the various outlets.

A media release is usually a one-page document that communicates what your product or service is about. A good media release should include a great headline and hook to make journalists pay attention to what you have to say. This is where some of your discarded titles and subtitles could come in handy.

The advantage of getting this kind of publicity is that it's free, as compared to advertising.

Always be on the lookout for newsworthy opportunities in the media. Although they're not interested in how you wrote a book, even though it's a huge achievement, if you can link your topic to how you can help their listener or viewer, you're more likely to be interviewed on TV or radio. You need to give your book legs!

My second book, *Ms Millionaire*, appeared on primetime morning TV. Funny that the first time it was meant to air was when Oprah announced she was coming to Australia, and the next time we were bumped for footage of floods that were devastating S.E Queensland. When it finally did air, I sold about three-hundred books and had writer's cramp from filling out all of the postage envelopes. So even if you have setbacks, be patient.

2. Social and Online Media

Social media allows you to partner with billion-dollar companies.

These days you can publish and promote your book with what's in your pocket. You have access to exactly the same distribution methods that in the past were only reserved for the big-name publishers, and best of all they're FREE. You can even publish on a range of platforms. These are some online media sites you can use to promote your book:

◆ YouTube

I like to call this your free TV network. It's your international broadcasting station. A good idea is to make a video series about the chapters in your book. Your potential client can watch you on their computer, tablet

83

or smartphone any time of the day or night. You create a channel and produce a piece once, and it becomes evergreen content people can watch over and over.

YouTube acts a big search engine like Google does, so you can spread your content across multiple platforms.

◆ Book Stores

Amazon, iBooks, Smashwords, Booktopia, and multiple other sites, are ready and waiting to sell your book. The biggest publishing platforms in the world now have no barrier for authors to publish their book and make it available worldwide.

They already have your ideal reader going to their website to look for the information contained in your book. These platforms are connecting readers with authors around the globe twenty-four hours a day, seven days a week. They take the order and look after the shipping and handling for you.

Most of the time it doesn't cost any money to have your book sitting in their store. It can also add a lot of credibility when people Google you and see you as a published author on Amazon. You can even have your own author page on their website. If you'd like to view mine, go to https://www.amazon.com/Fiona-Jones/e/B00HV0II74.

◆ iTunes

Consider iTunes your own radio station that allows your audio or video message to be broadcast to your ideal audience's back pocket. They can listen on demand. You choose the length of your segment and whether you want to record information from your book or interview others who work in your industry. Podcasts are becoming a popular way to share your message quickly and easily and increase your *author-ity* factor.

◆ Online Newspapers

With the changes in technology, more and more traditional newspapers are going online. Their model is changing, and they're looking for content creators to provide the articles for their publications. It much easier to go to the *author-ity* in an industry for an article than to find someone to interview. This means it's important for you to continue to publish more than just your book For instance, you can post blogs and write guest articles on other websites.

3. Mouth Media

Traditionally, an author's best marketing has been word of mouth, and the good news is that it's now amplified by the internet.

New authors can get their name out there and build their author platform by offering their book for free. This is a great way to share your message, but it needs to be part of an overall strategy. There are Facebook pages where you can download and add free e-books to let readers know about your book. Amazon Kindle Direct Publishing (KDP) has a KDP Select program that offers a free e-book to their readers, but you have to remain exclusive with Amazon for ninety days.

Writing *e-zine* articles, guest blogging and podcasting can be great ways for people to find out about your book. In fact, I often purchase books after hearing the author being interviewed on a podcast. When you become an author, the opportunities for being interviewed definitely open up. There are sites that match up podcasters with interviewees, so take action and get the word out.

There are so many ways to get your message out there. But smart promotion is key, so make it an important part of your strategy and overall purpose.

The Ripple Effect

When you become an author, you need to accept that you can change the life of someone you may never meet. Not everyone who reads your book will become your client, but they can become a fan for life, because you changed their life.

I live on acreage, where somehow one little pony became five horses. As I'm the person who usually picks up the poo, I decided it was time to sell two of them.

A lovely local lady came to see my horse and ride in the arena. When she lifted up the boot of her car to get her helmet, I couldn't believe my eyes. Sitting there, facedown, was a copy of my *Ms Millionaire* book. When I asked about it, she proceeded to tell me she'd read it on the plane coming back from the UK and told me how fantastic it was. She went on to say how inspired she was and that I should read it. I wasn't quite sure whether I should admit to being the author or not, but in the end I told her.

She wound up buying the horse and adjusting him at our farm, which meant I didn't have to part with him, and we became friends. This is what's known as the ripple effect. As people share your book with friends and family and tell others about it, they help spread your message.

Building Your Author Platform and Brand

Before deciding on a name for your business, you might want to check on sites like www.namechk.com that will allow you to find out what domain names and social media sites are available or already in use, without having to check on individual sites.

Once you get this in order, you can begin building your platform and brand.

▶ Your Brand

Your brand is a lot more than your logo. It's your methodology in dealing with clients or customers from their first contact with you.

When I had a waxing salon, we always used the greeting, "Ciao Bella", since the name of the salon was Bella Brazilian. Before long, the clients would repeat it back to us.

The logo, signage, website, water bottles and reusable tote bags were a big part of the brand, but what we became known for was the vibe and 'feel' that was created in the salon with the music, laughter and chit-chat. This is the reason we never introduced massage, as a quiet and relaxing salon we were not.

Here's another example to illustrate how crucial the element of vibe is for the brand. We once had a *Millionaire* party book launch held at an amazing private home on the Gold Coast waterfront that had in-floor fish tanks and a full open professional kitchen, with the chef cooking incredible finger food. The Moët flowed all night long. It might not have had the same impact had it been held in a back room of a conference centre.

Branding is also important in all of your communications. For the Millionaire books and school, I signed off every email or phone conversation with, "Thanks a Million!" Clients and customers loved it and soon adopted it for themselves. I sent birthday cards every year to contributors of the book series with sayings like, *You're one in a million* or *A million happy returns*, and thank you cards with *A million and one thanks*. Even now when I find some fantastic cards at the shops, I buy up all they have. This is in addition to our own custom-designed cards.

It caught on, and people used to email me back and write, *Thanks a Million!* I still smile when it happens. It's the power of putting detail like that into your branding.

When sending out emails, remember to include your company name alongside your own. If you met a potential client in a professional atmosphere, they may only associate you with your company. It's all about context. It still astounds me when I get an email from someone I don't recognise, because they neglected to include their company name. This kind of behaviour guarantees their email will wind up in the spam folder.

Your brand is about everything associated with you and your company. This includes your posts, your language, and your authenticity.

▶ Your Platform

◆ Author Website

Your author (*author-ity*) website and book sales page will promote your book and give you a platform for book sales. This is where you direct media and readers to find out more about you.

When you're building a business and a brand, it's vital to have an online presence as part of your author platform. If you're even considering traditional publishing, you should know that publishers will look you up to find out your niche before they take the time to read your manuscript.

Your author website should be a reflection of your book and include the following pages:

- ▶ home
- ▶ about the author
- ▶ buy the book
- ▶ products or services you offer, including speaking
- ▶ contact information
- ▶ your blog

Most WordPress sites have a simple plug-in for a PayPal shop to make it easy for people to purchase your book. Images of your book are also essential, so make sure you use professional graphics to position yourself in the best possible way. Also make sure to include links to your social media and any YouTube or other platforms where people can find your videos and information on your topic.

You've spent so much time and effort to produce a great book, so make sure all areas of your online presence are in alignment with your message. If someone were to Google you today, what will they find? Not having a social media presence or website displaying you as an *author-ity* means your message could be lost.

Your author profile is just as important as your book cover, so make sure your message is congruent. If you've written a book about staying healthy and fit, then you don't want your potential readers and clients finding pictures of you on Facebook partying the night away. Make sure that anyone looking up information on your products or services is directed to professional sites where they can learn more about you and purchase your book.

The first step to building a website is having a domain name, such as www.AuthorExpress.com. Some people choose to build their brand on their own name. Even if you're not ready to have a website, it's a good idea to register one under your name anyway, usually because over time, even if you change your niche, your name remains constant.

You can buy domain names inexpensively, usually around ten to fifteen dollars, from a domain name provider like GoDaddy, Crazy Domains or Hostgator, to name a few.

In the case where someone already owns the domain name you want, you can offer to purchase it from them. People will usually sell it to you anywhere from hundreds to thousands of dollars.

You may decide on another name if you can't secure the one you want. For example, if your business is in Australia, you can register under .com.au. If you can get both the .com and the .com.au, that's even better.

Setting up a site is easy on WordPress. They have templates. All you need to do is add your information and graphics.

You'll want to build of list of subscribers who are interested in your topic area and can potentially become customers. This means your website should include a way to capture a visitor's details, but you need to give something of value in exchange. On my website, people can sign up to get a free author starter pack. This means that when someone enters their name and email, I send them an e-book and five-part video series to get them started on their author journey.

In this way, I continue building a relationship by adding value and offering information in the form of a newsletter, blog posts, videos and webinars, as well as products and services. This function is known as an opt-in or subscriber box, and is commonly found at the top right-hand corner of a website.

You don't need to reply to each subscriber. You'll just need to set up an autoresponder message that replies automatically and provides them with what they've requested, such as a link to a free e-book or video series. An email marketing service like MailChimp can be used to capture the names and email addresses and also send emails and autoresponder messages.

Your offer will depend on your product and service and how your audience likes to consume information, whether it's audio, video or e-book.

◆ Social Media Sites

Securing these sites with the same name as your business name and URL is an important part of branding.

Consider securing vanity URLS on social media platforms. To secure one, such as www.facebook.com/YOUR COMPANY NAME, you need a minimum of twenty-five people to like your page.

Having a Facebook fan page is a great way to get started building your online presence and brand before you construct a website, but make sure you secure the domain name(URL) for later use.

Technology is always changing, For instance, Facebook now has Facebook Live, where you can stream videos in real time.

Take advantage of these tools. They will help you connect with and grow your audience. .

For YouTube, you need to have a minimum of a hundred subscribers to your channel before you can secure a channel name. Pinterest, Twitter and Instagram are much easier, since they can be yours if they're available.

As technology continues to emerge, more opportunities will arise for those wanting to boost their income, influence and impact on the world.

Author Action Steps

→ Come up with three enjoyable methods you'd employ to build your author platform.

→ Consider securing your name as a domain name.

→ Look up namechk.com to see if the domain name and social media sites are available.

→ Jot down the types of media that may provide the best approach for you to employ in your niche. For example, is your audience more likely to listen to your podcast, watch your videos on YouTube, or both?

PART TWO
Your Business

"Have the courage to follow your heart and intuition. They somehow already know what you truly want to become."

— **Steve Jobs**

Business is about how many people you can be of service to, not how much money you can make. The more people you help to get what they want, the more you get what you want. In other words, switch to thinking your business exists to solve problems and find solutions, and it will succeed.

Whether you're thinking of starting a business with a book, or expanding an existing business, I would like to share some of my own experiences to demonstrate how you can have a business you love.

What Business Do You Have or Want?

There's no better feeling than taking a little bit of inspiration and turning it into a real-life creation, whether it's a book, a building or a business. I've created all of them. You might find it more fun and a better use of your time to plan your next holiday, but if you create the life you want, you wouldn't need to take a holiday from it.

For me, I needed to start a brick-and-mortar business to know I didn't want to be controlled by when to have the doors open. In property development, there were too many variables such as the weather, the market, holding costs and building delays, and there was no guarantee of a sale at the end. My current business gives me the exact lifestyle I want with the income and flexibility to do what I love, working the hours I choose.

There are basically two business types: lifestyle and asset.

The type of business you want will depend on how you define success. If you want to be a stay-at-home mum and be there for your kids, then a lifestyle business may be just what you're looking for. Thanks to outsourcing, it's possible to work from anywhere in the world that has an internet connection.

Others dream of an asset business with big offices and heaps of staff who create products to sell. This is usually where the business isn't reliant on the founder to deliver the product or service.

Babies to Brazilians to Books

I've been the author of more than just books. I love being creative. Starting with a blank canvas and turning an idea into something real.

This is the definition of an *author-ity*.

It's the same reason I love assisting people with turning their knowledge into a real book they can hold in their hands. I can see the pattern of all of the pieces fitting together to bring me to where I am now in my journey. If life were a ten-chapter book, I'd be at chapter five.

I've dabbled in real estate and farming and now make a career out of publishing. At this point I'm an *Authorpreneur*, which is a combination of an author and an entrepreneur.

Recently I was on vacation in Hawaii. Now, I'm not sure if it was getting hit smack in the chest by a falling coconut, which by the way was unbelievably painful and took my breath away, but after this incident I realised for the first time that I'd actually created three businesses to date, and each of them had generated six figures in the first twelve to eighteen months.

I had zero experience before starting each of these businesses. In fact, my university degree was in medical imaging. I spent the majority of my career doing obstetric sonography on pregnant women, which I loved with all my heart.

I'd read the book *Rich Dad Poor Dad*, and although I was highly paid in my career, I knew I was swapping time for money, and I learnt that if I wanted to achieve real wealth I would need to have a business and other investments.

So along with investing in property and creating wealth through renovating small boutique developments, I decided to start a business.

So many people advised me not to undertake this endeavour. I was told I had no business experience, didn't have any staff and that most businesses fail. Running up against this kind of negativity made me more determined to succeed, and I really felt it was all going to be okay. I felt inspired to create a business, and nothing anybody said could stop me.

Business doesn't need to be complicated, and you don't need any certificates or qualifications to get started.

This is my journey from Brazillians to books.

▶ **Business #1: Beauty Salon**

I was living on the sunny Gold Coast where everyone wears bikinis, when the idea of owning a specialist Brazilian waxing salon came to me. I decided to set up and create a brand and a business. After heaps of brainstorming, the name and logo, *Bella Brazilian*®, was born.

I then set out to find a shop and some beauty therapists, even though I had not one single client at the time. I'd read lots of books, though, and found out that most people tend to buy themselves a job rather than building or creating a business. This taught me that my goal was to work on my business and not in it.

I found a great location surrounded by lots of trendy cafes, restaurants, and hair salons. It was a vacant, modern shop that had previously been home to three failed businesses. I used the negotiation skills I learnt from property investing to negotiate a great commercial lease, even though I'd never done this before and didn't fully understand the option terms, which I later found out added a lot of value to the business.

The owner of the shop lived interstate and didn't know about the local road works that were severely affecting the area, forcing several businesses to close. In my (basic) business plan, I explained about this and other factors that led to my offer on the rent, rather than just presenting a figure plucked from the sky. I was both excited and a little bit fearful when the owner agreed, and we signed the lease. As a new business owner with no experience, I wasn't able to get a business loan, so I redrew on one of my mortgages to fund the fit-out.

The shop was great. It was in an excellent location and space, so we decided to make it into a six-room salon. An architect friend designed the interior for me, and my husband and a builder got together and did the fit-out at a fraction of the cost of a shop-fitting company. This allowed us to buy the best salon software package available at the time with a great database system, which enabled us to text clients, a practice that's now commonplace.

I also negotiated every item we had to purchase for the salon and *tried* not to get emotional over whether the disposable underpants were pink or white (pink is my favourite colour, but the pink ones were ten times the price, so forget it).My property renovating experience taught me that every cent I expended would affect the bottom line. After employing our first beautician, we decided we wanted to keep her, and she needed money, so I employed her until we opened. She did anything we needed her to, from painting and cleaning to shopping for knick-knacks.

I paid her from my own wage as an ultrasonographer, until we actually opened. At that time I was reading *The E-myth* and *Think and Grow Rich* by Napoleon Hill, and what I learned is that I needed to imagine myself providing the product or service, getting a return for it, and state what I wanted the turnover to be in dollar amounts.

I did just that. I imagined happy customers feeling great and all of the fifty-dollar notes going into the cash till. You can imagine my surprise when the turnover for the first year was exactly what I'd written down, even though I'd never thought of it again.

The salon took off from day one, thanks to good old-fashioned service that outclassed our competitors, and some unique marketing strategies. One of the best ideas we had was to give our clients a bottle of water after their treatment.

The water bottles had our hot pink logo and contact details. People would refill them and use them over and over, and we used to get new clients phoning and saying they got our number off a friend's water bottle. The clients also loved receiving the complimentary water after their visit, as most stores were charging about three dollars at the time.

I loved my time in that business. The experiences I had and the people I met have led me to the path I'm on now. The financial reward after selling the business, that resulted from an offer too good to refuse, allowed me to spend the following three years doing whatever I liked. Had I not listened to my own inner voice and let myself be swayed by the opinions of others, I would have missed out on this experience.

The salon has recently celebrated its eleventh birthday, and I feel proud every time I drive by to see its longevity and the continued success of the new owner.

▶ **Business #2: Published Author/Entrepreneur**

I had an injury due to the nature of my work as a medical ultrasonographer, which meant I had to leave the career I loved. I went in search of something I could do to replace that income, and I attended a bunch of free seminars. At one of them, the speaker said that everyone has a book inside of them. I had no desire to write one, but the idea that you could create a business from a book, or add a book into a business, excited me.

Without knowing what I was even going to write about, I made a decision to invest $25,000 in my education and become a published author.

What I found through attending those free seminars was that I was in love with the story behind how the speaker started with nothing and created wealth.

The seed was planted to create the *Millionaire* book series and later the *Millionaire School*®.

Once again, I was in a situation where I had zero contacts and didn't know anyone to interview. I just started searching on Google and in business magazines. It was crucial I get over my fear when I started the book series, as I had to contact people who were on the *BRW* rich list and ask them to be featured in my book.

Getting over rejections and going outside of my comfort zone happened more times than I can remember. This is what I love about business. It's real-life personal development, because you suddenly have to acquire skills and ask for money and generally create something from nothing.

I had a system where I could sell copies of the books before I even printed them, so I was able to fund the entire project. I had an outcome and a strategy from the start. The series would be about the business behind the books and not just selling them.

I published nine books in that series and have inspired a lot of people along the way by sharing success stories. As an extension of the series, I formed the *Millionaire School®*, which is a platform for me to share my mentors with others. I loved my *Millionaire* journey and have met so many amazing people who've become lifelong friends.

The initial idea to franchise that business didn't progress as planned, and as time went on I came to realise it wasn't a business model that excited me. In fact, my goal was to use this valuable information and fold it into my next business, which was a lot more exciting to me.

▶ Business #3: Author Express

My third, and current, business, *Author Express®*, came about from constantly being approached by people who wanted to write and publish their own book. After helping over a hundred people become published authors through the *Millionaire* book series, I realised I was meeting the demand of a hungry audience of people wanting to become authors. This was about taking the story that's inside of everyone and showing them the exact steps to get it into the world in the form of a published book, which is something I absolutely love doing.

I developed an education program called *Author Express: From Inspiration to Publication in 5 simple steps*. Below is an infographic of the simple five-step system.

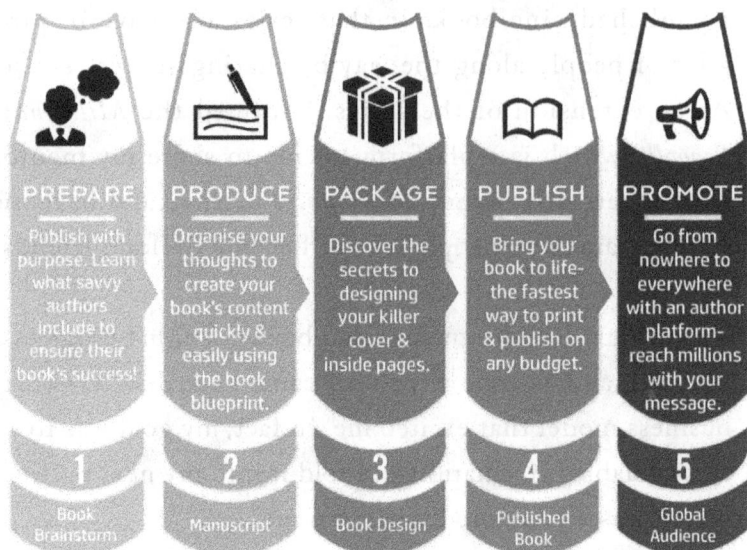

PREPARE — Publish with purpose. Learn what savvy authors include to ensure their book's success!

PRODUCE — Organise your thoughts to create your book's content quickly & easily using the book blueprint.

PACKAGE — Discover the secrets to designing your killer cover & inside pages.

PUBLISH — Bring your book to life- the fastest way to print & publish on any budget.

PROMOTE — Go from nowhere to everywhere with an author platform- reach millions with your message.

1 — Book Brainstorm

2 — Manuscript

3 — Book Design

4 — Published Book

5 — Global Audience

Author Express
From Inspiration To Publication In 5 Simple Steps

For more details on each of the five steps, go to *www. authorexpress.com* and download your free copy of the *Author Express Blueprint: The Ultimate Guide to Create, Publish and Promote Your Book.*

The name *Author Express* ® came about after heaps of brainstorming on the desired outcome. One was for people to become published authors, which is the *Author* part of the name. The *Express* part has a dual meaning. One has to do with the fastest way to publish a professional book (meaning

108

not just an e-book), and the other was for the author to express themselves and share their unique message, story or expertise.

We have a range of products and services under the *Author Express* brand to suit the needs of our clients that results in a professionally published book. I see a lot that aren't professionally published and haven't been designed in a way that will grow a brand or a business. This can do the same kind of damage as sending out poor quality video or audio. While being a perfectionist isn't a requirement for attracting quality clients, it's important to produce quality products.

When a book is published in a way that best represents who you are and what you offer, it can position you for amazing media exposure and act as a leveraged asset in your business, much like you'd receive from a professionally designed website consisting of educational material. You can then follow that up by using your book as a launching pad for seminars, workshops, retreats, and consulting and speaking gigs. The list is endless!

Once the book is complete, I encourage my authors to learn the art of repurposing the information by producing an e-book, audiobook and perhaps even a podcast to extend their audience reach.

That's why I love this process so much. What you're putting out is so much more than a book. It's the transformation you experience in the process of becoming an author, which is much like the journey of becoming a millionaire. But it's not about the money. It's about who you become in the process. So many people get incredible clarity, whether they have an existing business or use the book to start one up, as they go through the *Author Express* system. They come to understand it's all about that big vision and making sure the book is positioned for the business behind it. In other words, it acts like a *business card*.

As I like to say, it's not about *selling* a book, it's about *having* a book. Being a published author affects your position and credibility. In effect it means customers and clients seek you out. You've become the go-to person in your niche, since you're the author of the book. These days, having a book is the new black.

If you want to learn more about how you can become a published author and cross it off your bucket list, feel free to grab my free author starter pack at *www.authorexpress.com*.

I would love to help you join the dots and show you the exact steps to get that book out of you and into the world.

▶ Business #4: The Sky's the Limit

While I have no immediate plans to create another business at this stage, since I get my creative fix by helping others publish their book, I know for sure that whatever I do in the future will be a combination of my passion and serving others. To me, having a business and creating a brand is about a niche group of people who want to hang out with you and learn what you know, and then are inspired to help others do the same. The more people who can start doing what they love and showing others it's possible, the better the difference they can make in the world. Fulfilment comes when you ask the question, "How can I serve?" not "How can I make money?" I believe everyone is ultimately looking for a life of fulfilment and meaning.

Getting back to being hit by that coconut, I can say that along with realising how many successful business I've had, my epiphany was also about how I'm doing what I love and that all of my businesses have been about living my passion rather than focussing on making money.

Branding a Business with a Book

I love seeing authors branding their book alongside their existing business. The reason is that they've already spent a lot of time, effort and energy on their logo, website and design, and there must be a reason they've decided to align themselves with these images. I've seen people publish a book that's not at all aligned with their brand, and it's not nearly as effective.

I'm not saying the result has to be exactly the same, but the customer/client or reader feels safer when they're familiar with the look and feel of your business. Your book can be a great extension of your product suite. If you have an existing business, consider transitioning your brand into your book to maintain the look and feel of it.

Those who teach how to publish a book often come from the writing aspect of it and may not have a big-picture vision of your business, such as why you started it and how your book can fit into the bigger picture. What winds up happening is that the cover and content don't match your message. You need to have an overall strategy and use your book as a tool in your marketing kit.

When I produced the *Millionaire* books and created the *Millionaire School*®, my intention was to build a business behind the book, so it was important that the website, as well as social media, have consistent branding.

An exit strategy is an important part of any business plan. If you've been clear on your branding, when the time comes, it will make selling your IP, trademarks and domain names much easier.

The Business Behind the Book Method

A strategy that works well is knowing that your book is the start of your mini monopoly or empire. It's not important at this stage to have your entire plan created. It's more about planning to have the choice of building beyond the book.

One of the best methods is to unpack what you already do, such as your system or process of your product or service, and break it down into steps. If you can form an acronym or begin each step with the same letter, you'll be assured people will remember your message. My AUTHOR system is a good example of the acronym method.

- ▸ **A**-ction you want the reader to take as a result of your book.
- ▸ **U**-nderstand your readers' problems and how to solve them.
- ▸ **T**-each the reader by sharing pertinent information.
- ▸ **H**-elp- solve the readers' problems.
- ▸ **O**-utcome of the book, which is the reason you're publishing it.
- ▸ **R**-eader who's ideal for the information you're providing.

Producing a shape or image, such as my *Author Express* 5 Step System, adds to this degree of organisation and is an important way of communicating to the part of the brain responsible for decision-making. Having an image that represents your system means you can have a nice visual representation to include in brochures, on websites, presentations and your book.

Using my system as an example, here are the ways I utilise the five steps:

- For interviews or live speaking engagements as the five subjects I talk about
- The chapters of my book
- The modules in my workshop manual
- The framework for a podcast series
- Blog categories on which I can expand
- How I structure my webinars.
- The core topics for my introduction video series
- The way I structure my emails in an autoresponder series
- The way I structure my content on my blogs and YouTube channel

Skinny Series

Depending on the topic, you could expand your steps into a skinny books series. Each book would cover one of the major steps, and then each of these books is its own mini-*bookopoly*. What I love about this method is that it gets traction.

The author completes the first book and offers seminars, workshops and retreats around this one niche. Then the next book covers the following step in the process. This means you're constantly releasing new content for which you already have a built-in audience who will purchase it to consume the next part of the process. Now you have various products to offer instead of one signature product. New clients aren't necessary, and you're offering added value to your existing client base.

With this method you can hit the ground running sooner, as you only have to cover one step in the process and get to market faster.

Using my *Author Express* system as a skinny series example, I could have a five-part book series with these titles:

- ‣ Planning Your Book
- ‣ Producing Your Book
- ‣ Packaging Your Book
- ‣ Publishing Your Book
- ‣ Promoting Your Book

This method can be successful across many genres. For instance, a property developer can have a six-part skinny book series that acts as a business card for each step in the development project. The books can be Financing, Building, Buying, Selling, Development Types, Design and Decoration. A health practitioner could use this method just as easily, with the subjects Healthy Eating, Exercise, Energy and Breathing Techniques.

The topics covered are dependent upon the methodology or system of the individual practitioner. It's all about how you organise and order what you know. It means you have a business card for cooking and health retreats. What better way to go away to an amazing location than with people who've read your book and want to learn more from you, all while you get paid to do it? Think about how to turn your process into a book series and the product lines you can associate with it.

Repurposing

After you've spent the time and effort to produce your book, you can then start to repurpose and leverage it.

Your books content can then be turned into:

- an e-book
- an audiobook
- a Webinar presentation
- an interview framework
- a presentation
- a retreat
- a workshop
- guest articles
- blog topics
- podcast topics

As I said, I'm able to utilise my five-step system across a lot of platforms.

Promotional Partners

This is one of the best strategies for professionals, consultants and practitioners, and a great way to use a book to help grow your business by referral. This method relies on a referring partner or joint venture, where you supply copies of your book to someone who's successful in your area of expertise, and they hand it out to their clients as a way to refer clients to you. For example, if you're a mortgage broker, you supply a real estate agent with copies of your book to give to clients requiring finance. This way the real estate agent is able to bestow a valuable resource to the person buying the property, and the mortgage broker has a potential new client to serve.

Remember, this partner is not a competitor but someone who complements you and has the same client base. Who knows? You could end up running information sessions or workshops together. This has certainly occurred between authors in my *Author Express* program and those in my *Millionaire* book series.

You have to think of your book as a business and not be afraid to ask others to join you. It could lessen your load and create a mutually beneficial working relationship.

Mail Outs

Mail outs can work with promotional partners, as well as to your own contact list. What better way to let a client or customer know you value them than sending an autographed copy of your book? This is a great strategy for a skinny book, because for the same cost as a good gift card, you can print in bulk and easily post a copy to them.

Another option is to approach someone who again has the same target audience but is not in a competitive field, and ask them to send an email to their clients offering a free copy of your book. Now you've been granted access to their client list.

Establishing communication in the form of a free book will represent massive value to them and brand you as an expert.

Pre-sales

Before your book is even printed, you can start selling it wholesale in exchange for placing the buyer's contact information on the back. This is a great way to receive funding to offset publishing costs.

Another way is through crowd funding, such as gofundme.com and kickstarter.com.

Bulk Sales (pre or post-print)

I've utilised bulk sales by sending books to seminar companies whose main client base is my target audience. This can be win-win, as the seminar company can hand it out as a prize or include it in a gift bag to attendees. This allows you to get copies of your book into the hands of people who can join your email list, and the promoter has a product with a high perceived value compared to what they paid. Offering copies on a sliding scale is a good idea. For example, you can break it down like this, with different price points for each:

- ▶ 100-250 copies
- ▶ 250-500 copies
- ▶ 500-1000 copies
- ▶ 1000+ copies

Sponsorships

One of my authors, who works in the financial service industry, reserved a part of the back cover for a sponsor, who then added their logo and used the book as a client gift. This is a win-win-win for the author, sponsor and client.

Another author sold her inside cover to a company that's a supplier to her direct target audience, who then used it to advertise their services. Again, this is another way to offset printing costs.

What you can also do is something called white labelling. This is where you provide the content for the book, and your sponsors can add the book cover that will most appeal to their target audience. This can work in areas such as healthcare, real estate or mortgage brokering, where a book may have the face of the company or an individual acting as the author of the book, in order to grow their *author-ity* in their niche.

Subscriptions

A method that's been successful for my authors is using their books as subscription offers for national magazines. The way this works is that the book is used as a promotional tool to entice subscribers to renew for another year and in return get a free book. Again, this gets your book in the hands of people in your target audience, and the magazine gets more renewals. When both sides benefit, everyone wins.

Presentations

If you run workshop or give promotional talks, try using your book as a giveaway for attendees for signing up.

If you don't want to use it as a giveaway, you can offer your book or book bundle for sale at your seminars. This is a way to further your message of inspiration. You can even include it in your speaker contract as part of the deal, which means the event promoter or organisation where you're speaking needs to purchase a certain amount of books.

Often someone attending your presentation may also want to book you to speak at their event, so what better way is there to give them your details than personalising a copy of your book for them?

Create Opportunities

Eliminate excuses and take action! Get creative. The opportunities won't just land in your lap because you've published a book, but doors will open if you work smarter and partner with successful people and businesses to get leverage. The wrong way to market your book is to sit and peddle individual copies at a book fair.

I've had people tell me that it's fine for me to give this advice, since I have so many connections. But like I said, when I started I had no knowledge of the industry. My career in obstetrics didn't teach me about the seminar industry or who the key players were.

The answer is always getting your book into the hands of people with whom you can create opportunities.

Making a Million-Dollar Business

If you want a million-dollar business, reverse engineer it. If you're looking to add a book as an additional income stream, work out your current revenue versus your goal. It's simple math. If you're earning $250,000, you'll need to find a way to accrue an additional $750,000 to reach your target.

This can seem like an astronomical task. You don't want to feel defeated before you've begun, so it's a good idea to break down your goal into smaller, more achievable milestones you can accomplish along the way and keep you motivated. A good figure to start with might be $100,000.

In order to reach that target, you would have to sell:

- ▸ 100,000 e-books at $1 each
- ▸ 5,000 books at $20 each
- ▸ 1,000 products at $100 each
- ▸ 100 workshop spots at $1000 each
- ▸ 50 online programs for $2000 each
- ▸ 20 speaking gigs at $5000 each
- ▸ 10 high-end coaching packages at $10,000 each

Your business should be made up of a combination of these products and programs you can then break down into monthly revenue and plan your sales and marketing around your goal.

Maybe you don't want a million-dollar business. Some entrepreneurs have this goal in mind and realise they're more than happy earning $100,000 working from their home office. This is why breaking it down is a good idea. It all depends on what success looks like to you. What's important is that you participate in activities you absolutely love and get paid for doing them, while helping others to achieve the same outcome.

I no longer focus on money as a goal but instead the amount of people I can help become authors, because it's more meaningful and inspiring to me. As I said, I don't believe you should do anything purely for money. However, I would also agree that receiving money as a gift of appreciation from those you help achieve their dreams and as a measure of your results, is a great way to look at earning it.

Author Action Steps

- ➔ Get clear on what type of business you want.

- ➔ Have a concrete vision of the business behind your book.

- ➔ Come up with a specific call to action you want to leave with your reader.

- ➔ Consider which part of your platform you'd like to start with.

LAST WORD

I hope my last words inspire you to write your first.

Before you create your book, reflect on your life experiences, because there are no mistakes. Every step you've taken on your journey has brought you to this point, and if you're reading these words, it most likely means you're ready. It's time for you to share your knowledge, experiences and message with the world. You're already qualified. Too many people dream of publishing a book and never do it, because they let doubts and fears creep in. I've covered the five steps from inspiration to publication. There are only two important steps you need to take on your author journey: to start and to finish. Worrying about the details will keep you frozen. Take the leap and know there's going to be solid ground beneath you.

Find a mentor who's done what you want to achieve, so they can help guide you through the steps. This will save you time and costly mistakes. Remember, being a perfectionist means your book will die inside of you. Trust that once you take that first step, you'll soar and wonder why you didn't start sooner. You'll gain such a sense of accomplishment seeing your word count increase. Don't use your poor typing skills as an excuse! There's so much technology out there, you can walk around getting other tasks done and just talk your book.

Do you have a book inside of you waiting to come out? I know you do. Don't let fear stop your dream of becoming a published author. Set aside all excuses, limiting beliefs and any insecurities you might have about writing. Don't be that person who always says, "One day, I'll write my book." Get that idea and start writing. And remember: finishing is where the magic happens, so see it through.

Share Your Message| Make a Difference | Leave a legacy

MEET FIONA

Fiona Jones is a nine-times best-selling author who's worked closely with hundreds of Aussie entrepreneurs.

She's the creator of the *Millionaire* and *Elevate* book series, and founder of the boutique publishing company *Author Express* that helps people share their message with the world through the written word.

It's her love of reading and passion for inspiring people that led her to write her first book with a vision to develop a series.

Her mission is to inspire millions to *Be Their Own Success Story* by sharing her own inspiring stories through her books, as well as those by her *Author Express* members.

Connect with Fiona and Author Express

I would love to stay in touch and help you connect the dots.

More information and inspiration can be found on my author platforms below.

Website: www.authorexpress.com
Facebook: www.facebook.com/authorexpress
Twitter: @authorexpress1
Instagram: @authorexpress1
Podcast: www.authorexpress.com/podcast
YouTube: Search *Author Express* for Express Author Tips

Grab Your Free Author Starter Pack

www.authorexpress.com

Want to be an Author-ity?

There is simply no better way to increase your credibility and grow your business, than by publishing a book.

We love turning your IP into a professionally published book.

Our *Author-ity* process is for those who:

- ▸ *Want a book, ASAP!*
- ▸ *Have the IP or message to share*
- ▸ *Wants someone else to do it ALL*

We would love to help!

To find out how you can have your own customised book without doing all the work, then contact us today at www.authorexpress.com/IP.

Author Express
From Inspiration To Publication In 5 Simple Steps

www.ingramcontent.com/pod-product-compliance
Lightning Source LLC
Chambersburg PA
CBHW071657210326
41597CB00017B/2227